W9-DIG-426

BEING IN THE TEXT

BEING IN THE TEXT

Self-Representation from
Wordsworth to Roland Barthes

PAUL JAY

 CORNELL UNIVERSITY PRESS
Ithaca and London

Cornell University Press gratefully acknowledges
a grant from the Andrew W. Mellon Foundation that aided in bringing
this book to publication.

Copyright © 1984 by Cornell University Press

All rights reserved. Except for brief quotations in a review, this
book, or parts thereof, must not be reproduced in any form without
permission in writing from the publisher. For information address
Cornell University Press, 124 Roberts Place, Ithaca, New York 14850.

First published 1984 by Cornell University Press.
Published in the United Kingdom by Cornell University Press Ltd., London.

International Standard Book Number 0-8014-1599-3
Library of Congress Catalog Card Number 83-45145

Printed in the United States of America

*Librarians: Library of Congress cataloging information
appears on the last page of the book.*

*The paper in this book is acid-free and meets
the guidelines for permanence and durability
of the Committee on Production Guidelines for
Book Longevity of the Council on Library Resources.*

Dedicated to the memory of C . L . Barber

Contents

Acknowledgments 9

Introduction 13

The Question of Genre 14

Writing, Psychoanalysis, and the Problem of the
Subject 21

From Wordsworth to Barthes: The Historical
Argument 32

O N E   The Wavering Balance: Wordsworth's Journey
through *The Prelude* 39

The Philosophical Moment: Hegel and the Aesthetics
of Self-Creation 42

The Theory of *The Prelude* 46

The Composition of *The Prelude* 59

T W O   Something Evermore About to Be: "Wordsworth" and
the Poetics of Revision 73

Repetition, Recollection, and the Art of Forgetting 74

From Blindness to Insight 83

THREE   **Carlyle and Nietzsche: The Subject Retailored** 92

Sartor Resartus and the Mystification of
Autobiography 94

History as Dramatic Narrative 108

FOUR   ***A Portrait of the Artist as a Young Man*:
The Art of Fictional Self-Representation** 115

FIVE   **Self-Representation and the Limits of Narrative** 141

Joyce and Proust: The Theory of Fictional
Autobiography 142

The Education of Henry Adams: Multiplicity, Chaos,
and the Self-Reflexive Experiment 153

SIX   **A Strange Mimesis: The Discourse of
Fragmentation** 161

Paul Valéry's *Moi*: Self-Representation as
Auto-philosophy 163

T. S. Eliot's *Four Quartets*: Retrospection and the
Poetry of Deferral 168

Roland Barthes's *Roland Barthes*: Disorder and the
Destiny of the Subject 174

Index 185

Acknowledgments

This book has benefited in countless ways from the suggestions of those who read portions of it in its various stages of development, and I am pleased to be able to acknowledge my debt to them. Thomas Vogler and Hayden White provided valuable support and criticism in the early stages of its writing. The suggestions of James Olney were extremely helpful in revising portions of the manuscript. Deborah Kaplan also read a draft with great care, and her generous suggestions and criticisms were invaluable in giving shape and focus to my argument.

Others provided material assistance that made possible the completion of this work. Paul Skenazy kindly furnished me with office space when I needed it most. Lynn Galiste, Irene Baldron, and Terry Atwell typed parts of the manuscript. A fellowship from the Regents of the University of California enabled me to take time off from teaching to write much of it. I could not have asked for a more patient or skillful editor than Bernhard Kendler. His good sense contributed in many ways to the present form of this book.

Finally, I thank my wife, Lynn Woodbury, for her encouragement and support during the time I was writing. She took time off from her own writing to read portions of this work, and her perceptive comments and keen editorial eye saved me from many an embarrassment. The quality of our life together made the book possible. Material from Chapter 6 appeared in a somewhat different form in *Modern Language Notes*. Reprinted with the kind permission of Oxford University Press are excerpts from William Wordsworth's *The Prelude or Growth of a Poet's Mind* (Text of 1805), edited by Ernest de Selincourt and corrected by Stephen Gill, copyright 1970 by Oxford University Press; excerpts from *The Poetical Works of William Wordsworth*, edited by Ernest de Selincourt and Helen Darbishire, copyright 1949 by Oxford University Press; and excerpts from *The Prose Works of William Wordsworth*, edited by W. J. B. Owen and Jane W. Smyser, copyright 1974 by Oxford University Press. Excerpts from *Four Quartets* by T. S. Eliot are reprinted by permission of Harcourt Brace Jovanovich, Inc., and Faber and Faber Ltd.; copyright 1943 by T. S. Eliot, renewed 1971 by Esme Valerie Eliot. The lines from Kenneth Burke's "Hypothetical Case" are reprinted from his *Collected Poems, 1915–1967*, copyright © 1968 by Kenneth Burke, by permission of the author and the University of California Press.

PAUL JAY

Atlanta, Georgia

Being in the Text

Suppose you called into the darkness
Or across a valley at midday
Or through the woods
Or down a corridor, for that matter—
And got your answer.
Then what?

KENNETH BURKE, "Hypothetical Case"

Introduction

This book surveys the evolution of literary forms from the Romantic to the Modern period in which authors make themselves the subjects of their own works. The variety of self-reflexive works here examined permits a twofold analysis. On the one hand, what follows is a discussion of the psychological, spiritual, philosophical, and vocational uses to which autobiographical literary modes have been put. This discussion, however, is subservient to the book's larger aim, which is to analyze historically the impact of changing ideas about both the psychological "self" and the literary subject on the forms of literary self-representation in the nineteenth and twentieth centuries. It thus views self-reflexive literature from Wordsworth to Barthes from a historical, philosophical, and theoretical perspective: historical because it articulates the evolution of differing literary strategies for creating such a form; philosophical because it traces this evolution as an adjustment to a changing epistemology of the subject; and theoretical because it centers on the theory of composition that animates and sustains the works of each of the writers considered.

The Question of Genre

While all of the works discussed in this book are to some degree autobiographical, it is not my aim to define a literary genre called "autobiography" nor do I attempt to outline a subgenre of like-minded autobiographical works. Consequently, while my interests are partly historical, I do not attempt to create the history of a literary genre. My focus is on the evolution and not the categorization of self-reflexive literary forms in the nineteenth and twentieth centuries. While each of the works treated here in some way reflects, or reflects on, the autobiographical act, and while all of them are commonly included in studies of autobiography, none claims our attention primarily as a factual, objective life-history. Thus, while taking their autobiographical qualities as my point of departure, I resist the idea that the works can be categorized as "autobiography" in any coherent or helpful way.

Indeed, the attempt to define autobiography as a literary genre is attended by a number of problems. The question of such a definition has concerned critics interested in the form ever since its relatively recent emergence as a serious topic for literary studies.[1] The problem, put succinctly by James Olney,

1. In a somewhat arbitrary way, this interest might be dated from the publication of Roy Pascal's *Design and Truth in Autobiography* (Cambridge: Harvard University Press, 1960). In the last ten years the study of autobiographical literature has flourished. For a fine discussion of the emergence of autobiography as a popular topic for literary studies, see James Olney, "Autobiography and the Cultural Moment: A Thematic, Historical, and Bibliographical Introduction," in *Autobiography: Essays Theoretical and Critical*, ed. James Olney (Princeton: Princeton University Press, 1980), 3–27. Pascal's book provides a good overview of the genre question as confronted by critics of autobiography. Two more recent book-length studies of this question are Elizabeth W. Bruss, *Autobiographical Acts: The Changing Situation of a Literary Genre* (Baltimore: Johns Hopkins University Press, 1976), and William Spengemann, *The Forms of Autobiography: Episodes in the History of a Literary Genre* (New Haven: Yale University Press, 1980). For a comprehensive bibliography of critical and theoretical works on autobiography, see William Spengemann, "The Study of Autobiography: A Bibliographical Essay," in *The Forms*

is that "everyone knows what autobiography is, but no two observers, no matter how assured they may be are in agreement" about *what* it is.[2] Why? Because, Olney suggests, the great majority of works classifiable as autobiography were written under a host of different conventions all of which predate what we can only in *hindsight* begin to call "autobiography." Thus, Olney asks why in recent times autobiography seems to be being "practised by everyone" and answers, "perhaps this is so because there are no rules or formal requirements binding the prospective autobiographer—no restraints, no necessary models, no obligatory observances gradually shaped out of a long developing tradition and imposed by that tradition on the individual talent who would translate a life into writing."[3] For Olney, long a leading critic in the field, "autobiography" is a mode of writing that can be infinitely varied. There may be, he writes, "no way to bring autobiography to heel as a literary genre with its own proper form, terminology, and observances."[4]

Though critics may argue at length about a generic definition of autobiography in the abstract, the problem begins in earnest when we move from defining the genre to listing the actual texts it includes. It is one thing to say, for instance, that an autobiography is a factual and more or less objective life-history of its author that includes details about personality and emotional, spiritual, and social development, and quite another to insist that *The Prelude* and *The Autobiography of Benjamin Franklin* belong to the same genre. A strict constructionist

---

of Autobiography. This bibliographical essay will be an indispensable tool for students of the form. The essays collected by Olney in *Autobiography: Essays Theoretical and Critical* also provide a very valuable introduction to the literature on the subject.

2. Olney, *Autobiography*, 7.
3. Ibid., 3.
4. Ibid., 4. For the articulation of this view, see Olney's essay, "Some Versions of Memory/Some Versions of *Bios*: The Ontology of Autobiography," 236–67. Also see his earlier book, *Metaphors of Self: The Meaning of Autobiography* (Princeton: Princeton University Press, 1972).

might exclude *The Prelude*, since in the first place it is a poem and in the second it explicitly relies upon the imagination. But can we argue that Franklin's *Autobiography* is any less constructed than Wordsworth's poem? Franklin's "life" in his autobiography is mediated by both the opportunities and the limitations of narrative. Is there any real sense in which the life therein is ontologically less a literary constuction than is Wordsworth's in *The Prelude*? Clearly not; the difference is in degree, not kind. But if we do include both works under one heading called "autobiography," what possible value does such a designation have? To what set of rules do they both adhere? If, however, we define "autobiography" so as to exclude *The Prelude*, how much sense would this designation make?

The point here is that while Franklin's *Autobiography* is less consciously imagined and poetic than *The Prelude*, it nevertheless presents a life shaped by the exigencies of narrative art. Franklin's autobiography may strive to be more detailed, controlled, chronological, and objective than Wordsworth's but since it is a narrative and not a "life," it is a literary creation, as much an aesthetic construction as Wordsworth's. Such a linkage, moreover, clearly associates both texts with any artistically conceived narrative, no matter who its subject may be. This is why the attempt to differentiate between autobiography and fictional autobiography is finally pointless. For if by "fictional" we mean "made up," "created," or "imagined"—something, that is, which is literary and not "real"—then we have merely defined the ontological status of any text, autobiographical or not. Again, moving from the abstract to the concrete clarifies the problem. If we remove the words "factual" and "objective" from our definition of autobiography, we create a genre in which a work like *A Portrait of the Artist as a Young Man* co-exists with Frank Lloyd Wright's autobiography. Now this juxtaposition may or may not make sense from an ontological point of view, but its value for literary studies is certainly limited. Despite the many compelling and convincing arguments for categorizing fictional autobiographies like Joyce's (or Proust's) as autobiography, to do so defines a genre so impossibly large as to be worthless. For what novel cannot be read autobiographically and thus categorized as an autobiography? Such a consideration recently led William Spengemann to insist that *The Scarlet Letter* was Hawthorne's "autobiography"— albeit an autobiography that, he writes, represents a "non-biographical program for autobiography."[5] If, indeed, *The Scarlet Letter* may be generically termed an autobiography by virtue of such a program, then perhaps Paul de Man's ironic definition of autobiography is correct, and any "text in which the author declares himself the subject of his own understanding," any text, that is, "with a readable title-page is, to some extent, autobiographical."[6]

5. Spengemann, *Forms of Autobiography*, 132. Spengemann's attempt in this book both to define autobiography as a genre and to chart the "episodes" of its historical evolution (the word "episodes" perhaps indicates a healthy uneasiness about such an attempt) exemplifies the pitfalls inevitably encountered by such a project. His aim is to posit a history of autobiography that at the same time will define the genre. Thus, in tracing the genre's evolution from a "historical" form to a "philosophical," and finally, a "poetic" one, he attempts "to chart the formal permutations that, all together, constitute what autobiography is" (xiv). Spengemann takes the "permutations" of autobiographical form which make its generic definition so difficult and in effect asserts that together they *constitute* the genre. In fact, in the modern period, this genre comes to encompass virtually *every* literary text: "Autobiography thus becomes synonymous with symbolic action in any form, and the word ceases to designate a particular kind of writing. To call any modernist work 'autobiographical' is merely to utter a tautology" (168). The problem with Spengemann's formulation is not so much that it is wrong but that it creates a *genre* out of such disparate works as Augustine's *Confessions*, *La vita nuova*, *Sartor Resartus*, and *The Scarlet Letter*. Such a genre is implausible at best. Spengemann's historical argument does resemble the one I make in the present work, but I differ fundamentally with, among other things, the assertion that the books treated in either study constitute a genre.

6. Paul de Man, "Autobiography as De-facement" in *MLN* 94 (December 1979), 921–22. De Man's essay is a concise and logical discussion of both the pointlessness of trying to define autobiography as a genre and the concomitant attempt to decide which works do and do not fit into it. Implicit in de Man's analysis of autobiography is a kind of deconstructive strategy drawn from Der-

The main problem with treating autobiography as a genre, then, is that it raises questions which, as de Man succinctly puts it, are both "pointless and unanswerable."⁷ There will always be the temptation in defining autobiography as a genre either to create borders that are too exclusively narrow or ones that are so large as to be meaningless. And if the border between autobiography and fiction is erected on a privileged notion of referentiality, then the study of autobiographical works will always be partly founded upon an illusion. De Man makes a very fundamental point about such an illusion:

> Are we so certain that autobiography depends on reference, as a photograph depends on its subject or a (realistic) picture on its model? We assume that life *produces* the autobiography as an act produces its consequences, but can we not suggest, with equal justice, that the autobiographical project may itself produce and determine the life and that whatever the writer *does* is in fact governed by the technical demands of self-portraiture and thus determined, in all its aspects, by the resources of his medium?⁸

De Man rejects the idea that the subject in an autobiographical work represents a privileged form of referentiality. He wants, instead, to view the subject as a textual production. What we always confront in any autobiographical work, he argues, is not a series of historical events but a series of efforts to write something. The action proper to autobiography, he insists, is not historical but rhetorical.

If, then, there is a problem with treating any of the works discussed in this book as if it belonged to the genre of autobiography—or, indeed, with treating any work as autobiography—

---

rida. For a book-length consideration of autobiography, drawing on the theories and methods of contemporary French critical theory, see Jeffrey Mehlman, *A Structural Study of Autobiography: Proust, Leiris, Sartre, Lévi-Strauss* (Ithaca: Cornell University Press, 1974).

7. De Man, "Autobiography as De-facement," 919.

8. Ibid., 920.

there is also the difficulty of treating the works in question as if they belonged to *any* single genre. For instance, the work included here that seems most clearly to fit the simplest accepted criterion for autobiography—an author's attempt to render his own life-history—is in fact much more than an "autobiography." Although Henry Adams' *The Education of Henry Adams* goes into great detail examining in chronological fashion the life-history of its author, it is written in an ironic tone in the third person and is laboriously interested in issues seemingly peripheral to autobiography: political and social history, the rise of science and technology, and its author's own complicated "dynamic theory of history." While this work seems closer to autobiography than anything else, it would not serve well as a defining example for such a genre.

Of the other works in question here, two seem most comfortably defined as novels: Joyce's *A Portrait of the Artist as a Young Man,* and Proust's *A la recherche du temps perdu.* Neither, however, is in any sense a conventional novel, not least because of their insistent autobiographicalness. Each in its own way transforms the nineteenth-century novel of education into something at once more autobiographical than the *Bildungsroman* and yet more self-consciously aesthetic. Each is often cited as integral to the emergence of the modern novel, but in significant ways they relate to the tradition of the novel by violating its conventions.

The other self-reflexive works treated in this book are even more difficult to categorize generically. Wordsworth's *The Prelude* is very often treated as an autobiography, but its clearer roots are in the epic. And yet it is obviously not an epic concerned with the same landscape as, say, *Paradise Lost.* If Wordsworth's poem is an epic it is an epic of the inner life and thus different in kind from Milton's. Geoffrey Hartman prefers to describe *The Prelude* as a "verse-epistle," which considerably complicates the question of genre; are we then to classify Wordsworth's poem with *Clarissa* rather than with Rousseau's *Con-*

fessions? If we can say one thing for certain about *The Prelude*, it is that the poem defies categorization by genre. This can be said with even greater certainty of Carlyle's *Sartor Resartus*, a patchwork parody that subverts any attempt to create for it a generic pigeon-hole large enough to hold any other work. Paul Valéry, of course, sought to avoid restrictions of genre altogether with his vast *Cahiers*, and while he deemed them to be in part autobiographical, they are impossible to categorize as autobiography, or even as memoir. And finally, *Roland Barthes by Roland Barthes* is a book of fragments arranged alphabetically, and its seeks, while being self-referential, to be an anti-auto-biography. Written to be a locus for Barthes's "resistance" to his own ideas, it is a book in which, he says, all must "be considered as if spoken by a character in a novel."[9] Least of all a novel, and only by the most generous of definitions an autobiography, Barthes's book (which perhaps has Pascal's *Pensées* as its major precursor), really belongs to no genre.

What finally connects each of these works is their tendency to transgress the norms of the genre with which they seem most closely allied. All are "major works" in the sense articulated by Tzvetan Todorov: "The major work creates, in a sense, a new genre and at the same time transgresses the previously valid rules of the genre [with which it is most closely allied]. . . . One might say that every great book establishes the . . . reality of two norms: that of the genre it transgresses, which dominated the preceding literature, and that of the genre it creates."[10]

---

9. *Roland Barthes by Roland Barthes*, trans. Richard Howard (New York: Hill and Wang, 1977), frontispiece.

10. Tzvetan Todorov, *The Poetics of Prose*, trans. Richard Howard (Ithaca: Cornell University Press, 1977), 43. Jonathan Culler has the same idea in mind when he writes: "The expectations enshrined in the conventions of genre are, of course, often violated. Their function, like that of all constitutive rules, is to make meaning possible by providing terms in which to classify the things one encounters. What is made intelligible by the conventions of genre is often less interesting than that which resists or escapes generic understanding, and so it should be no surprise that there arises, over and against the *vraisemblance*

Linked as they are by their transgressions of generic boundaries, each work examined in this book finally defies generic
categorization because the psychological, literary, and philosophical needs that animate their authors raise problems of
presentation that impel them to seek fresh modes of composition
beyond the bounds of any particular inherited one.

This largely explains why each work seems to have no identifiable poetic or novelistic precursor. I will argue that this is so
because each work develops out of its author's confrontation
with a particular problem—the problem of literary self-representation. Each of the texts in question represents its author's
efforts to produce a self-reflexive literary work within a changing
epistemology of the subject—in both the psychological and
literary senses of the word. Viewed together they illustrate the
evolution of changing ideas about the literary subject in self-
reflexive literature from the Romantic to the Modern period. I
treat them together here not to establish the history of a literary
form but to chart the evolution, and attempted resolution, of
such a literary problematic. In each case, the author's confrontation with himself, his attempt to make himself the subject
of his own book in ways consonant with his own ideas about
subjectivity and its literary representation, situates the work in
the history of an on-going problem: how to use one medium—
language—to represent another medium—being.

Writing, Psychoanalysis, and the Problem of the Subject

The analysis of literary self-representation which follows is
double-edged: it charts the evolution of proliferating textual
strategies for self-reflexive literary composition as they emerge
in response to changing conceptions of the subject; and, at the

---

of genre, another level of *vraisemblance* whose fundamental device is to expose
the artifice of generic conventions and expectations" (*Structuralist Poetics:
Structuralism, Linguistics and the Study of Literature* [Ithaca: Cornell University Press, 1975], 148).

same time, it examines the psychological, spiritual, and vocational uses to which these strategies are put. These two levels of analysis will unfold side by side because in the self-reflexive literature of the period in question the problem of the subject as an ontologial construct is always conflated with the problems that the autobiographical subject is seeking to both depict and resolve in his text. That is, the personal imperatives animating a work like *The Prelude* appear in Wordsworth's poem as a set of problems whose resolutions become complicated by the poetic and compositional difficulties that plague its construction. Since Wordsworth comes to identify the successful completion of the poem with the successful resolution of the spiritual and vocational problems that animated it, the difficulties encountered in its composition both mirror and complicate these problems. It is for this reason that my historical study will move continuously between the philosophical and the psychological, from examining problems inherent in literary self-representation to examining the personal needs that animate the subject who writes about himself.

While the historical, psychological, and philosophical levels of my analysis will unfold simultaneously, I want, at the outset, to distinguish between them. The historical matter of this study is of course literary. The "history" in what follows is the history of changing textual forms for literary self-representation. This should be clear from even a cursory look at the table of contents. The psychological and the philosophical levels of the analysis are somewhat more complicated, however, especially in their specific relation to the historical developments being charted.

If all writing is a form of self-analysis, then autobiographical writing is probably the most *explicitly* self-analytical. The "psychological" level of inquiry in this study will thus be concerned with how various modes of autobiographical writing represent different forms of self-analysis. The analytical function of self-reflexive composition may be obvious, yet we cannot simply identify such a function as central to the many kinds of works

we call "autobiographical" and then leave it at that. For historically, as we shall see, the temptation to indulge in such analysis
has been difficult either to resist or to carry out successfully.
Since my examination of the analytical function of works like
The Prelude and *A la recherche du temps perdu* will hinge
on their parallels with the psychoanalytic process of Freud's
"talking cure," it is important to sketch in that relationship at
the outset.

Freud acknowledged that poets discovered the unconscious
before he charted it, and it is equally clear that autobiographical
writers as different as St. Augustine and Wordsworth discovered
the psychoanalytic process before Freud himself practised it.
The psychoanalytic function of the process of self-reflexive composition is explicit in Augustine's *Confessions*, and a brief look
at its resonance with Freud's talking cure will introduce this connection, one that will figure prominently in our examination of
self-reflexive writing from Wordsworth to Barthes.

While Augustine's book has been conventionally understood
as the story of his life prior to the book's composition—the
story, that is, of events leading up to his conversion—it is in
fact every bit as concerned with his renewal and transformation
as he writes it. From the outset, Augustine exists in his own
narrative less as a subject to be remembered in language than
as a subject to be transformed by language. Begun some ten
years after his dramatic conversion in the garden at Milan, the
Confessions begins with Augustine lamenting that his soul now
"lies in ruins"; in writing his book, he hopes that God will help
him to "build it up again."[11] He writes of the past in order to
"heal" in the present what he calls his "infirmity" (262). One of
his central purposes in writing, then, is to perform a healing
kind of self-analysis. His goal *while writing* is to "bring back" to
his "mind" his "past foulness," so that "in the bitterness of . . .

11. St. Augustine, *The Confessions of St. Augustine*, trans. John K. Ryan
(New York: Image, 1960), 46. All further references to this work appear in
parentheses in the text.

rembrance" he might reexperience the "sweetness" of God, a
process which he hopes will "gather me together again from
that disordered state in which I lay in shattered pieces" (64).
In the *Confessions*, then, Augustine's past transformation is
recalled in order to help effect a similar one in the present;
"Augustine" the subject of the *Confessions* is linked to Augustine
the author of the *Confessions* in a labor of representation which
seeks, by recalling the former, to transform the latter.

The explicit connection in the *Confessions* between retrospection and introspection is what signals the link between the
process of its composition and the processes of psychoanalysis.
The text's double preoccupation is reflected in its division into
two parts, the retrospective narrative of Augustine's life (Books
1–9), and the introspective exegetical portions that follow (Books
10–13). This division does not represent a break in the book—
as many critics have argued—it marks Augustine's transposition
of the story of his past spiritual journey to the topography of his
present inner life.[12] The latter portions of the book do not break
with the former; they extend Augustine's self-analysis into the
very present in which he is writing. By turning his focus, at the
opening of Book 10, from "what I once was" to "what I am now,
at this very time when I make my confessions" (231), Augustine
simply makes explicit the connection between the two aspects
of his self-analysis—retrospection and introspection. Moreover,
this shift makes clear that in composing his *Confessions* he is
quite consciously involved in the on-going therapeutic process
of attempting to heal the infirmities of his soul.

Augustine's intermixing of narrative confession and discursive
self-analysis in a specifically therapuetic venture is what aligns
his textual project with the methods of Freud's talking cure.
The whole idea of a cure in psychoanalysis, of course, depends

12. For a summary of this critical debate, see R. S. Pine-Coffin's intro-
duction to his translation of the *Confessions* (Penguin, 1961). See also John C.
Cooper, "Why Did Augustine Write Books XI–XIII of the *Confessions*?" in
Augustinian Studies 2 (1971), 37–46.

on the subject's ability to fashion a narrative, a discursive formulation of the meaning of past events identified *in* the process of analysis as significant. It is both the linguistic ground and the creative potential of such a retrospective process of introspection that connects the narrativizing in an autobiographical text like Augustine's with the narrativizing at the very heart of the psychoanalytic process.

Of course, what is crucial to the transforming power of the talking cure is Freud's recognition of its doubly creative nature. The subject's cure is bound up in the ability to participate in generating a creative story in which key recollections are linked to form a therapeutic autobiographical narrative. However, the past events recollected in such a process may not in fact be "events" at all but, rather, imagined moments in a "history" being created in and by the act of analysis itself. As Freud recognized in his discussion of the "Wolf Man" case, recollections "brought up by an exhaustive analysis" may not be "reproductions of real occurences," but rather, "products of the imagination . . . which are intended to serve as some kind of symbolic representation."[13] This, he insists, is a "fact": "scenes" from the past "are not reproduced during the treatment as recollections, they are the products of construction."[14] This recognition, he insists, should not "alter" the "carrying-out of analysis . . . in any respect": "The analysis would have to run precisely the same course as one which had a *naïf* faith in the truth of the phantasies."[15]

Freud's point here is that the past represented in analysis is both a discursive and a symbolic one. The material recollected is less a "pure" past than a narrative created in the present as the subject imaginatively reworks conscious and unconscious

13. Sigmund Freud, *The Standard Edition of the Complete Psychological Works of Sigmund Freud*, trans. James Strachey (London: Hogarth, 1955), 17:49.

14. Ibid., 50–51.

15. Ibid., 49–50.

material. It is the present perspective of the subject that contains the key to the "symptoms," and that can authorize and enact the cure. Jacques Lacan's insistence on the discursive nature of the talking cure is instructive in this regard: "What we teach the subject to recognize as his unconscious is his history— that is to say, we help him to perfect the contemporary historization of the facts which have already determined a certain number of the historical 'turning points' in his existence."[16] For Lacan, recovery in analysis depends on the subject's creation of a self-reflexive discourse that can historicize conscious memory into an eventually "perfected" narrative. The process of perfecting this narrative becomes the vehicle for the subject's cure. Since the discourse is a contemporary historization, it is manifestly created and hence, in part, fictive. Thus the recuperative power of the narrative resides not in its factualness but rather in the creative capacity of language itself. Lacan's insistence that the cure in psychoanalysis is developed discursively is clearly tied to his conviction that "psychoanalysis has only a single intermediary: the patient's Word."[17] In his view, language is the base upon which the superstructure of a curative discourse is founded. The psychoanalytic process turns on the subject's formulation of his past into a narrative, not on the past itself, which really has no existence outside that formulation.

Lacan's characterization of the analytic enterprise is concisely descriptive of Augustine's attempt to create an autobiographical text whose very composition might allow him to gather himself together from a "shattered" and "disordered" state—to recompose and "heal" himself, in part, by composing an autobiographical work. We will see this same hope operating in Wordsworth's *Prelude*, but we will also see it undermined in

16. Jacques Lacan, *The Language of the Self: The Function of Language in Psychoanalysis*, trans. Anthony Wilden (Baltimore: Johns Hopkins University Press, 1968), 23.

17. Ibid., 9. For Lacan's elaboration of this assertion, see *Language of the Self*, 9–27.

later works as varied as *Sartor Resartus, Four Quartets*, and *Roland Barthes*. For while Augustine's attempt prefigures a central and repeated use of the autobiographical form, it also contains a set of internal contradictions that prefigures its undoing. This is because, as I have already noted, the personal and psychological goals animating a retrospective self-analysis like Augustine's—or Wordsworth's—nearly always become conflated with compositional and rhetorical problems at cross-purposes to those goals. The personal and psychological resolutions that these texts seek to mediate are often disrupted, or even displaced, by the aesthetic problems of translating a psychological subject into a literary one. Indeed, the writer's growing recognition of such a disruption, and his attempts to circumvent it, will be seen at the very heart of the evolution of the autobiographical strategies reviewed here.

If the content of many of the self-reflexive works treated in this study has its source in personal crises, the *form* of these works is determined in good measure by aesthetic and philosophical crises. This brings me to the other level of my historical examination, the philosophical. As I shall be arguing throughout, the tendency to formal experimentation within the general bounds of an autobiographical literary practice from Wordsworth on is in direct response to a changing epistemology of both the psychological and the literary subject. The concept here can be simply put. Augustine's belief that his soul is a unified—or unifiable—spiritual creation of an all-knowing God to whom, and to whose plans, he is subject, and to whose transcendent Word he has access, dictates that he produce a certain kind of autobiographical work. On the other hand, Carlyle's conception of the self as a thoroughly secular "moving rag-screen, over-heaped with shreds and tatters," "thatched" together "day after day" by a "despicable," "actual" person, dictates quite another kind of autobiographical work. The form of a narrative like the *Confessions*, that is, reflects and reifies a particular philosophical (or theological) conception of the subject, and the form of a book like *Sartor Resartus* reflects and reifies the unravelling of that same subject.

This unravelling surfaces intermittently in *The Prelude*, increases in *Sartor Resartus*, and finally becomes the dominant topic of *Roland Barthes by Roland Barthes*. Its clearest and most relevant philosophical articulation is in Nietzsche's critique of the subject in *The Will to Power*. This critique, summed up in his insistence that "the 'subject' is not something given," but that it is "something added and invented and projected behind what there is," has of course now become an axiom in contemporary literary theory.[18] Nietzsche's critique at once de-mystifies and problematizes the subject. His central and most crucial assertion is that the psychological subject is not an ontological given that exists before we invent or project it; he holds that the Western tradition of the "self" is just that—a constructed tradition. This "self," recognized as an epistemological construction, clearly for Nietzsche refers not to a natural, privileged, and potentially unified psychological condition, but rather, to a historically constituted set of ideas and assumptions whose referents are complexly dispersed within the very language we must use to think the self into being. Nietzsche's assertion, it should be noted, does not deny the fact of the subject's existence; it simply insists that the central fact about subjectivity is that its previous formulations have the status of a fiction, and that our own (particular and historical) role in creating that fiction must be acknowledged as more properly—and importantly—a "fact": "'The subject' is the fiction that many similar states in us are the effect of one substratum: but it is we who first created the 'similarity' of these states; our adjusting them and making them similar is the fact, not their similarity(—which ought rather to be denied—)."[19]

In Nietzsche's view, then, the notion that the self exists as a

18. Friedrich Nietzsche, *The Will To Power*, trans. Walter Kaufmann and R. J. Hollingdale, ed. Walter Kaufmann (New York: Vintage, 1968), 267.
19. Ibid., 269.

unified and pure spirit is contradicted by its purely discursive origins.[20] Hence, the dissimilarity between identity and discourse is understood as the epistemological context within which the self is produced, and its status as a product is what becomes central. Now, it is precisely this dissimilarity that is at work in disrupting the smooth transposition of the psychological subject of an autobiographical text (the author) into its literary subject (its protagonist). What I will be charting in this study of self-reflexive literature from Wordsworth to Barthes is the growing recognition of how complex and problematic such a transposition is and, in addition, how its disruption can in turn disrupt the personal and psychological goals of such works.

Nietzsche's philosophical critique of the subject is relevant here because it formalizes and makes concrete a suspicion alive in autobiographical literature at least since *The Prelude*. In its emphasis on the "invented" and "projected" nature of the self and on the discursive "adjustments" that give it at least the illusion of unity, it of course looks forward to a twentieth-century conception of the self. But on the other hand, it also focuses attention on the central contradiction that plagues any autobiographical text: the ever-present ontological gap between the self who is writing and the self-reflexive protagonist of the work. For we shall see that it is the implicit, or at times explicit, recognition of such a gap—and the author's consequent response to it—that in large measure determines both the method and the form of a work. In fact, the philosophical and aesthetic problems inherent in the recognition of such a contradiction often form part of the subject matter of autobiographical works.

Again, we can turn briefly to Augustine's *Confessions* to illustrate the point. We have already noted how the temporal break between Books 9 and 10 of the *Confessions* represents Augustine's shift from a retrospective to an introspective mode, a shift from narrative recollection to discursive analysis. What

20. Ibid., 266.

needs to be emphasized here is that embodied in the series of meditations which comprise the final four books is an analysis of the very instrument—memory—that sustains the first nine. For much of Book 10, through its analysis of perception, memory, and representation, calls into question the ability of language to mediate both its author's self-division and his estrangement from God. While the discussion here is philosophical rather than personal and retrospective, it in fact extends the self-analysis of Books 1–9 into the realm of the philosophical. That is, the topic remains Augustine himself and the maladies of his soul, but here the self-questioning turns to the complexities of his own mind. Now he has "become a riddle to" himself, "and *this* is [his] infirmity" (262, my emphasis).

Such a turn comes about because here Augustine becomes involved in an insistent examination of the contradictions inherent in his own self-reflexive project: "I truly labor at this task, and I labor upon myself. I have become for myself a soil hard to work and demanding much sweat. . . . It is I who remember, I the mind . . . what is closer to me than I myself? . . . [But] the power of my own memory is not understood by me, and yet apart from it I cannot even name myself" (245). The line of thought here is characteristic of much of Book 10: memory is understood as the requisite power for self-reflection and identification, and yet the process of remembering seems beyond Augustine's understanding. Thus subjectivity itself becomes a kind of conceptual riddle for the autobiographer in the autobiography. The self becomes, philosophically, a difficult labor, a "soil hard to work." Here Augustine's examination of the processes of cognition and representation has the effect of questioning the ontological status of the narrative portion of his book and the "I" who is its subject.

Crucial here is Augustine's focus on the inability of language to bridge the distance between what he takes to be a past self and a present self. This conceptualization has its roots in his insistence that memory cannot mirror things themselves but can only form "images" of them: "[T]hings themselves do not enter [memory], but images of things perceived by sense are kept ready there for the thought of the one recalling them" (237). Insisting that "we labor amid the remains of our obscurity" (337), Augustine understands the mind to be a "deep receptacle" (236), a "cavern" (246) full of "dark areas" (260) and "recesses" (271), in which he can be "deceived" (260): "Within me are those lamentable dark areas wherein my own capacities lie hidden from me. Hence when my mind questions itself . . . it is not easy for it to decide what should be believed." (260).

Augustine is wary in these passages of a double displacement of identity in the processes of cognition and recollection: in the first place "things themselves do not enter" the "great cave of memory," and then once displaced there, they surface in an act of self-consciousness which displaces their identity yet again. This double displacement, of course, has an important bearing on the status of the subject in Augustine's narration of his own past life, since he insists that "When true accounts of the past are given, it is not the things themselves, which have passed away, that are drawn forth from memory, but words conceived from their images." (291)

As a meditation on the philosophical problems underlying literary self-representation, Book 10 foregrounds the difficult "labor," the "hard work," of using language to represent being in a text. Augustine's labor reifies, if it does not anticipate, Nietzsche's notion that subjectivity must always be "invented and projected behind what there is," and it makes explicit— both in thought and action—the contradictions and difficulties that attend such a labor. While it stands, then, as an allegory *par excellence* of the Christian's soul's efforts to unite with God, it also stands as an allegory of the self-reflexive writer's problematic efforts to bridge the distance between past and present—between himself and his own textual representation of himself. Its assertion of a relationship between self-reflexive writing and spiritual transformation expresses the hope of any autobiographer who views this literary mode as a path to renewal. But at the same time, there may be difficulties as the path twists, zig-zags, and turns in upon itself.[21]

From Wordsworth to Barthes: The Historical Argument

I will, then, undertake my historical analysis by examining the changing uses of self-referential composition from the Romantic to the Modern period and by considering the ways in which evolving forms of self-reflexive literature responded to changing conceptions of the "self" and its status as a literary representation. I begin with *The Prelude* because there is no other self-reflexive work of the early Romantic period that more clearly articulates the potential uses of such a form, but which at the same time exemplifies philosphical and compositional

---

21. We should note here Augustine's belief that the mediating powers of the Word will save his autobiographical work from the ironies he confronts in its closing books. For Augustine, the story of his conversion to the Word in fact takes its power and its authority—that is, its efficacy—*from* the Word. This is why the language of the *Confessions* is so thoroughly permeated with the language of scripture. In composing his book, as Ryan points out, Augustine blended his own language and the language of scripture to form a single authoritative discourse (Ryan, 37–38). Representing the past in this way—translated into the terminology of scripture—Augustine felt he could transform the meaning of his own past life. By doing so, as Kenneth Burke observes, Augustine believed that the empirical events of his life could be elevated to a transcendent level, and the authority of his book guaranteed. Realized *in* his own text by virtue of that authority, the self who experienced those events becomes a transcending being. Here is Burke on this aspect of the *Confessions*: "The great store of Biblical texts, learned verbatim and spouted forth at appropriate moments [by Augustine], were like attitudinally slanted names for situations. Each time a situation arose, it presented itself to him in terms of some Scriptural formula that in effect adopted a policy with regard to it. Thus by confronting a current situation in terms of a Biblical response, such citations had the effect of making the situation itself essentially Biblical, to be classed with conditions not literally present at all. Thus there is a sense in which his Biblical terminology of motives enabled him to 'transcend' the sheerly empirical events of his time" (*The Rhetoric of Religion: Studies in Logology* [Boston: Beacon, 1961], 58).

problems that will extend well into the modern period. Wordsworth's poem recalls Augustine's hope that by writing a self-
analytical retrospective narrative the author might fix "the wavering balance of [his] mind" (*The Prelude* 1:650), but it also
anticipates representational dilemmas that, during the course of
the nineteenth century, will pressure writers working in a self-
reflexive mode both to call this hope into serious question and,
in the process, to seek new forms for such a mode beyond the
bounds of a strictly historical and biographical narrative.

Wordsworth was of course writing his poem at a time when
art, thought, and self-consciousness were shaking themselves
free from a specifically theological epistemology, and when what
Hegel called the "practical activity" of aesthetic cognition and
representation was itself coming to be thought of as a spiritual
and a self-transforming act. Thus in *The Prelude*, the spiritual
journey related in Augustine's *Confessions* is transposed into
the very activity of the poem's composition—Wordsworth's
"journey," that is, is less a retrospective story to be recounted
than a literary activity enacted as the author composes his poem.
"The growth of a poet's mind" does comprise its story, but the
growth is best seen unfolding in the process of the poem's
composition.

Because the poem is replete with meditations on the problems that confront its author as he writes it, *The Prelude* provides a unique insight into the paradoxes of literary self-representation in a period when the self was coming to be thought
of less as the creation of a deity and more as the construction
of humankind's own mental powers. This growing realization
represents the broad philosophical context in which Wordsworth's poem was born. It sanctions both the notion that Wordsworth's own poetic language can represent being and the hope
that in the very activity of representing that being he can transform it. In his pursuit of such a project we can trace a series
of ideas crucial to the autobiographical efforts of those who
followed him: that the writer's past contains a power to liberate

him from a debilitating spiritual and literary condition; that a chronological, biographical narrative self-analysis can help perform such a liberation; and that the power of his own creative language can, by transforming the past with which it is concerned, help transform the autobiographical protagonist who is its subject.

However, Wordsworth's poem also confronts a series of paradoxes that, as they threaten the efficacy of his restorative project, presage the historical undoing both of the hope which animates it and the representational premises upon which that hope is founded. Such an undoing is reflected in both the substance and structure of *Sartor Resartus*. While Wordsworth's autobiographical narrative has only moments of irony, Carlyle's treatment of Teufelsdrockh and his autobiographical scribblings is ironic throughout. The doubts, hesitations, dilemmas, and disappointments implicit in *The Prelude* become explicit in *Sartor Resartus* and are represented in the very form of Carlyle's book. Carlyle weaves a radical critique of the truthfulness, value, and efficacy of self-representation into the content and the structure of his book, and in Part 2 (the mock biography of Teufelsdrockh based on Teufelsdrockh's own autobiographical documents) he makes a mockery of the value of autobiographical information *per se*. Thus Carlyle's text consciously becomes the paradox that Wordsworth's poem intermittently encounters but seeks to avoid.

In both its author's comments about the patched together and fragmented nature of the "self" and in the disjointed quality of its discursive form, Carlyle's text reflects a retailoring of worn-out notions about both the psychological self and the literary subject. Thus, where Wordsworth seeks to forestall the dissolution of his subject in *The Prelude*, Carlyle gleefully enacts that dissolution in the very structure of his text. Wordsworth, that is, writes his retrospective narrative to order himself into a renewed state of unity, while Carlyle ironically represents the impossibility of such an effort by creating a mystified autobiography of himself that explicitly disorders and disperses its subject. In so doing, *Sartor Resartus* questions the efficacy of the ordering and the healing power of Wordsworth's poem and at the same time seeks to undermine the idea that the self is a "homogeneous little figure" that can be "tightly articulated" in a biographical narrative.

The kind of philosophical critique of the self that animates Carlyle's book (and disturbs its structure) is of course recurrent in nineteenth-century thought. Indeed, the evolution of autobiographical forms during this period is tied to such a critique, for changing ontological and epistemological theories of the self and its status in literary representation opened new creative avenues for autobiographical literature. While many continued to write traditional autobiographical narratives, Carlyle in his text can be observed prefiguring a split in the form which travelled in roughly two directions, one leading to the overtly fictional practices best exemplified by Joyce's *Portrait* and Proust's *A la recherche* and the other to a highly varied but always self-consciously discursive practice like that of Eliot's *Four Quartets* or Barthes's *Roland Barthes*.

Joyce's autobiographical practice makes systematic the Carlylean notion that literary self-representation is always already a form of self-fictionalization. Consonant as it also is with Nietzsche's insistence in *The Use and Abuse of History* (1873) that the "historical" is an aesthetic creation whose truth is dramatic rather than objective, Joyce's novel seeks to use the form of a fictional narrative to resolve the tension between fact and fiction encountered by Wordsworth. That is, Joyce seeks to dramatize the truth about his past by means of a fictional reconstruction rather than in and by an ostensibly historical recollection whose objectivity would be unavoidably compromised the moment pen was put to paper. Thus Wordsworth's intermittent realization that his autobiographical protagonist might in fact be fictional becomes for Joyce the willful strategy of composing his *Portrait* in the form of a novel. While the *Portrait* has a number of affinities with both *The Prelude* and Augustine's *Confessions*, Joyce's strategic decision to fictionalize his material is an effort both to sidestep the representational paradoxes inherent in Wordsworth's project and willfully to reverse the theological aims of Augustine.

Many of the theoretical assumptions underlying Joyce's book parallel those of Proust, whose *Past Recaptured* actually articulates a literary-psychological theory of autobiographical composition. On the surface Proust seems to posit a relationship between memory and self-renewal akin to Wordsworth's, so that his *Recherche* seems a vast (though vastly different) repetition of the Wordsworthian attempt to recollect privileged "spots of time" in order to renew himself in (and for) the present. However, Proust's elaborate fiction resists such a simple comparison, for the novel creates a patently fictional "Marcel." Rather than remember and re-present a past self, Proust willfully forgets the past in a literary operation that allows him to create an imaginatively conceived Other. The fictionality of Proust's (and Joyce's) text represents a putting to death of the past, a willful forgetting that is the pretext for its imaginative re-creation in what Eliot later called "another pattern." It is this paradox—that the autobiographical work has come to be based on conscious forgetting rather than on careful remembering and on fictional re-presentation rather than on historical presentation—that separates these modern narratives from their poetic predecessor.

The literary-historical development here is a simple one: the fictional mode of self-representation practiced by Joyce and Proust seeks to resolve the complex philosophical and structural ironies of *Sartor Resartus* by returning to a biographical narrative mode like Wordsworth's, but in a way that turns on its head the poet's attempt to faithfully picture his past. Chronological narrative remains as the structural principle of these works, but truth becomes a function not of remembering but of fictionalizing. These two autobiographical novels thus represent

a marked refinement of Wordsworth's secular and literary transposition of Augustine's *Confessions* but at the same time they
structurally retain the conviction that a self has a coherent biography that, since it constitutes it, must be re-told—whether
factually or fictively.

It is this conviction that gives way in the modern period to
a conception of the subject and its status in literary self-representation that has its sources in Carlyle's and Nietzsche's philosophical critiques. For the wholeness and coherence of the self,
the primacy of biography in self-representation, and the role
of narration in representing both, is undermined by a variety
of twentieth-century self-reflexive works whose preoccupations are more philosophical than biographical and whose subjects are represented in fragmented discursive forms that seek
by their fragmentation to mirror what modern criticism has
come to call (perhaps too simply) "the divided self."

Such works grew out of a self-conscious preoccupation with
the kinds of contradictions encountered at the turn of the century by Henry Adams as he composed his *Education*. Taking
Augustine and Carlyle as his precursors, Adams tried and failed
to marry narrative and discursive modes in the writing of his
book. His frank admission of the inadequacy of narrative as a
form for modern self-representation and his conviction that the
modern ego was a chaos of "multiplicities" looks forward to a
self-reflexive practice that articulates, and sometimes embraces,
such a chaos. Thus we find Paul Valéry representing his "moi"
in a series of fragments fashioned to reify his conviction that the
self is "composed of bits and pieces that have never coexisted."
Since he finds no sense of unity in himself, his self-reflexive
writing is purposely disunited, eschewing biographical narration
in favor of philosophical investigation. T. S. Eliot, on the other
hand, seeks in the *Four Quartets* for the unity Valéry has
abandoned, but his poem finally can only search in a repetitive
way for a kind of Presence it can never articulate. Eliot's journey recalls Augustine's, but the doubts he entertains about the

ability of his retrospective poetic project to complete such a journey align him more logically with Wordsworth. There is in Eliot's poem no systematic deconstruction of the self who is its protagonist but, like the protagonist of *The Prelude*, the poet's destiny is always "something evermore about to be," for it is tied to a rhetorical mode whose frailties leave him, like his fishermen, "forever bailing."

Abandoning narrative as a mode of self-representation, Barthes's *Roland Barthes* seeks by its fragmented form to be the systematic deconstruction that Eliot's poem avoids. This strange kind of mimesis constitutes the rhetorical logic of his book. Wholeness, unity, and especially "transcendence" are viewed by Barthes as "risks" to be avoided at all cost. He insists that the Wordsworthian conception of the self as a "single enormous network" is a wornout metaphor, that the subject today must be recognized as "divided," "dispersed," "contradictory," and without "a central core" or a "structure of meaning." Thus his *Roland Barthes* denies the recuperative hope of *The Prelude* and consciously seeks to reverse its nostalgic, ordering, and unifying strategies.

In its grappling with representational and philosophical dilemmas glimpsed and repressed by Wordsworth, Barthes's book makes clear how far modern self-reflexive texts have evolved in response to problems first raised by the Romantics—and anticipated long ago by Augustine. His deliberate attempt to order his work to reflect what he calls a "new knowledge" of the subject sets it apart from other self-reflexive texts that were only disturbed by the intimations of such knowledge. Additionally, his preoccupation with a kind of self-analysis which is less psychological than philosophical indicates how the psychoanalytic function of self-representation has gradually given way in the modern period to a consciously philosophical and deconstructive one. What follows, then, is an attempt to chart this gradual shift in both the form and function of autobiographical literature as it evolved in the nineteenth and twentieth centuries.

CHAPTER ONE

The Wavering Balance: Wordsworth's Journey through *The Prelude*

> —Here must thou be, O Man!
> Strength to thyself; no Helper hast thou here;
> Here keepest thou thy individual state:
> No other can divide with thee this work,
> No secondary hand can intervene
> To fashion this ability; 'tis thine,
> The prime and vital principle is thine
> In the recesses of thy nature . . .
>
> [*The Prelude* 13:181–88]

"There clearly comes a time," Geoffrey Hartman has written, "when art frees itself from its subordination to religion or religiously inspired myth, and continues or even replaces these. This time seems to coincide with what is generally called the Romantic period."[1] Wordsworth's reminder to himself that in the "work" of composing *The Prelude*[2] he has had to provide

---

1. Geoffrey Hartman, "Romanticism and 'Anti-Self-Consciousness,'" in *Romanticism and Consciousness*, ed. Harold Bloom (New York: Norton, 1970), 52.

2. *The Prelude, or Growth of a Poet's Mind, 1805*, ed. Ernest de Selin-

strength for himself, that his own "individual state," and not a "secondary hand," has had to probe for his poetical powers in the recesses of his own nature, is an exemplary declaration of the kind of freeing Hartman has in mind. While M. H. Abrams is in part correct when he observes that *The Prelude* has Augustine's *Confessions* as its "ultimate source," Wordsworth's poem also has its sources in the philosophical thought of the Romantic period, a period in which art, thought, and self-consciousness were breaking free from "subordination" to an inherited theological tradition.[3] As Wordsworth's poetry certainly makes clear, the Romantic artist did not so much break with "spiritual" matters as transpose them into secular terms. With no "Helper," the poet is left with himself, divinity comes more and more to be identified with a privileged form of Nature, and the poet's abilities are perceived to come not from God but from within himself.

---

court, corrected Stephen Gill (Oxford: Oxford University Press, 1970). All references to *The Prelude* are from this edition and book and line citations appear in parentheses in the text.

3. M. H. Abrams, *Natural Supernaturalism: Tradition and Revolution in Romantic Literature* (New York: Norton, 1971), 83. Abrams understands *The Prelude* to be a secular version of the *Confessions*' specifically Christian "circuitous journey" to an "original" unity with God. He argues that Augustine's journey becomes "transposed" (chiefly under the influence of the German Idealists) into the plot of the writer's own journey of "progressive self-education," an education which leads the modern writer to "reconciliation and reunion" with his own "other" (179, 187). Abrams lumps *The Prelude* together with Proust's *A la recherche* and Eliot's *Four Quartets* (among others) in asserting not only the "theological" basis for their stories (83), but the *redemptive* achievement they represent for their authors. Abrams's linking of these texts is valuable, but he consistently forces the Christian model of fall and redemption on texts (like *The Prelude*, and *A la recheche*) that cannot really bear it, creating the illusion that a completed text is a completed redemption. In Christianizing the implications of whatever seems metaphysical in the texts, Abrams elides the complexity of doubts that attended their composition. In fact, the reunification and the redemption he reads into these texts is usually forced onto them by the paradigm he uses in interpreting them. The present study is in part an effort to correct Abrams's version both of what these texts seek to do and of what they are able to achieve.

That this transposition had a profound impact on the role and place of the subject in literary discourse is obvious. However, the specific impact of this transposition on self-reflexive literature has never been systematically worked out. And yet it in fact represents the philosophical context in which its various forms began to multiply. Set adrift from the notion of an absolute relation between the self and divinity and from the Augustinian belief in the mediating powers of a transcendant "Helper," a poet like Wordsworth puts pen to paper on the brink of a much more problematical task than that even of the author of the *Confessions*. The sense of Wordsworth's being at the dramatic edge of something difficult and dark resides between the lines of the passage quoted above: he "must be" alone with his own strength, "no other" can divide his work with him, there will be no intervention—it is as if the poet is at once proudly announcing and hoping against hope. In this thin tension resides the problematic hero, the divided self, the writer as the subject of his own work, who will come to be so persistent in modern literature.

The kind of transposition Hartman identifies is far from an easy one. He is clear on what he calls the "serious paradox" that attends the separation of poetry and religion for the Romantic writer:

> [A]s soon as poetry is separated from imposed religious or communal ends it becomes as problematic as the individual himself . . . for the artist is caught up in a serious paradox. His art is linked to the autonomous and individual; yet that same art, in the absence of an actively received myth, must bear the entire weight of having to transcend or ritually limit these tendencies. No wonder that the problem of the subjective, the eccentric, the individual, grows particularly acute.[4]

Wordsworth's paradox is like Augustine's, but the poet is without any divine "Helper." His "serious paradox" is that he must

4. Hartman, "Romanticism and 'Anti-Self-Consciousness,'" 53.

fashion his own ability to transcend himself: he must keep his individual state, must penetrate the recesses of his own nature, and yet without an intervening hand whose power is secondary, and thus above, or beyond him. *The Prelude*, documenting such an effort, is nearly an archetypal example of Hartman's formulation: Wordsworth's poem becomes "as problematic as the individual" who is composing it, and it becomes so precisely because that individual "must bear the entire weight of having to transcend" his own autonomy and his own individuality. Wordsworth's poem—written over nearly the whole first half of the nineteenth century—forges in this way an absolute link between Romanticism, the problematic subject, and the rise of autobiographical art as a self-conscious *literary* form.[5]

In its attempted transposition of divinity and its power to nature and the mind, Romanticism can be seen reformulating "divinity" itself. In this reformulation, art's task remains "religious," but only in the sense that it seeks *itself*—as art— to relocate, and re-articulate, what is true in a transcendant sense. The essential nature of this reformulation is elaborated by Wordsworth's great German contemporary, Hegel, in a way that makes explicit the implied kind of interaction between the mind, creative power, and divinity, which is reflected in Wordsworth's poem. Its resonance with Wordsworth's project is worth noting.

The Philosophical Moment: Hegel and the Aesthetics of Self-Creation

In *Vorlesungen über die Aesthetik* (1818), Hegel observes that art "no longer affords that satisfaction of spiritual wants which

---

5. While I have chosen to focus on *The Prelude* in my discussion of this problem as it begins in the Romantic period, one might also turn, of course, to Rousseau's *Confessions*. For a discussion of this work in the tradition of autobiography, see William Spengemann, *The Forms of Autobiography* (New Haven: Yale University Press, 1980), 62–72.

earlier epochs and peoples have sought therein."[6] Art, he writes, can no longer be "venerated as divine" (32); as a sensuous object embodying divinity, art "remains for us, on the side of its highest destiny, a thing of the past" (34). While Hegel asserts here that the *content* of art can no longer be viewed as divine, he does not abandon the idea of divinity in art. Rather, he relocates it in the *process* of artistic production, a process that can reflect the "deeper" "truth" of "spirit" (geist) itself (32). This "truth" is inherent for Hegel in the very process of thought: "Thought— to think—is precisely that in which the mind has its innermost and essential nature. In gaining this thinking . . . the mind is behaving according to its essential nature" (35). For Hegel, this "essential nature" is "spirit" itself. When a work of art is created by the processes of cognition and representation it is not the content of art but the creative nature of its materials' passage through the mind that gives it a "spiritual nature" (35–36):

> The work of art has no feeling in itself, and is not through and through a living thing, but, regarded as an external object, is dead . . . its external existence . . . is not what makes a work into a production of fine art; it is a work of art only insofar as, being the offspring of mind, it continues to belong to the realm of mind, has received the baptism of the spiritual, and only represents that which has been moulded in harmony with mind . . . This gives the work of art a higher rank than anything produced by nature, which has not sustained this passage through the mind . . . For everything spiritual is better than anything natural. At any rate, no existence in nature is able, like art, to represent divine ideals. [55–56]

Hegel, in essence, argues here for a *reversal* of the old notion that natural processes exhibit Divine production while man's

6. G. W. F. Hegel, *On Art, Religion, Philosophy: Introductory Lectures to The Realm of Absolute Spirit*, trans. J. Glenn Gray (New York: Harper and Row, 1970), 33. These "introductory lectures" were never published by Hegel but were collated with the aid of his students' notes for publication after his death. They were presented by Hegel each year from 1818 until his death in 1831. All further references to this work appear as parenthetical page numbers in the text.

creative capacities do not. "Not only," he writes, "is there a divinity in man, but in him it is operative under a form that is appropriate to the essence of God, in a mode quite other and higher than in nature" (56). Man's mind, Hegel insists, is the only medium through which "the divine element" can pass: "In the products of art God is operative neither more nor less than in the phenomena of nature; but the divine element, as it makes itself known in the work of art, has attained, as being generated out of the mind, an adequate thoroughfare for its existence" (56–57).

In Hegel's view, man's mind is the only "thoroughfare" or "passageway," the only "medium of existence," through which the "pure spiritual existence" of God can be represented. This formulation concisely exhibits the philosophical point of view out of which the Romantic (and modern) preoccupation with subjectivity, the "inner life," and the development of self-knowledge began to grow: "[I]n the mode of pure spiritual existence [God] is to be known as *mind* and in mind. His medium of existence is therefore essentially inward knowledge and not external natural form . . ." (106).

This mode of knowing has as its end the attaining of "the true notion of its [the mind's] absolute essence"; to do this, the mind "has to traverse a course of stages whose ground is in this Idea itself," a process in which "the mind as artist presents to itself the consciousness of itself" (106–107). It is this traversal that is exhibited in exemplary fashion in Wordsworth's retrospective search for self-knowledge in *The Prelude*, and it signifies for Hegel no less than "the universal and absolute need out of which art, on its formal side, arises" (57). In art this need, which "has its source in the fact that man is a *thinking* consciousness," is wedded to humankind's creative power, so that the traversal through "inward knowledge" becomes a self-transforming act. The artist, Hegel writes,

> draws out of himself, and makes explicit *for himself*, that which he is, and, generally, whatever is. The things of nature are only

immediate and single, but man as mind *reduplicates* himself . . .
is *for* himself, perceives himself, has ideas of himself, thinks
himself, and thus is active self-realizedness. This consciousness
of himself man obtains . . . for himself by *practical* activity,
inasmuch as he has the impulse, in the medium which is directly
given to him, to produce himself, and therein at the same time
to recognize himself. (57–58)

This "reduplication" is not simply a matter of mirroring: Hegel
views this "practical activity" as an act of self-transformation.
The "self" produced in this activity is different from the self
that began it. It is one "which he [the artist] does not leave as
he finds it but alters of set purpose" (58). The artist's "impulse"
is "to exalt the inner and outer worlds into a spiritual consciousness for himself, as an object in which he recognizes his own
self." In "this reduplication of himself" what "is in him" is "realized" as "vision" and "knowledge" (59).

It is this kind of realization that Wordsworth seeks in the
"practical activity" of "reduplicating himself" in *The Prelude*,
and as such his narrative actualizes the Hegelian project outlined in the *Aesthetik*. Hegel's formulation outlines the nature
of the historical moment out of which Wordsworth's narrative
was born. His idea that consciousness is "obtained" and is "realized" by "practical activity," that it is produced in and by language, looks forward to Nietzsche's thoroughly secularized assertion that subjectivity is humankind's invention. However, it
does so without explicitly recognizing the serious paradoxes
inherent in such an activity. For as long as Hegel can believe
that God can be "known as mind" by way of inward knowledge,
the practical activity of the self-reflexive artist seems to retain its
untroubled ability to "reduplicate" subjectivity as "pure spirit."

While Hegel's formulations *implicitly* make it clear why a
Romantic autobiographical poem like Wordsworth's can both
look back to Augustine's *Confessions* and forward to the modern
problematizing of subjectivity, Hartman's elaboration of Romanticism's paradoxical burden makes it quite *explicit*. Hartman
views the relationship between religion and art in Romanticism

as more schematic than thematic, since it resides primarily in the similar motif of the "journey" which informs both the story of the Christian pilgrim's "problematic crossing" from "death to second life or from exile to redemption" and the crossing of the Romantic poet from nature, and self-consciousness, to imagination: "The traditional scheme of Eden, fall, and redemption merges [in Romantic poetry] with the new triad of nature, self-consciousness, imagination; while the last term in both involves a kind of return to the first."[7]

This merging, as I have already suggested, creates the context for a problematic crossing for a poet like Wordsworth because he has no "Helper," no "Secondary hand"—he is severed, that is, from an Augustinian relationship to the Word, so that his own poetic language must bear the burden of his journey. Transposing the priest's journey into the poet's, *The Prelude* retains the Augustinian relationship between language, authority, and self-transformation, but it recasts the context within which it functions. Wordsworth's search is for a way to unite the self with *poetic* power, it is played out as he writes a *secular* confession, and it involves the search for an authoritative and powerful *poetic* language.

The Theory of *The Prelude*

A brief over-view of the aims and the structure of Wordsworth's poem will begin to reveal the "serious paradox" generated by such a search. As a poem that is searching for origins, *The Prelude* seeks to both enact the poet's return to the beginning, the source, of his poetic power and to reanimate an "original" lost poetic language.[8] This can be seen clearly in Wordsworth's essay, "Poetic Diction," which more than anything else outlines the larger boundaries of his poetic quest in *The Prelude*.

7. Hartman, "Romanticism and 'Anti-Self-Consciousness,'" 54.
8. On Wordsworth and the search for origins, see Leslie Brisman, *Romantic Origins* (Ithaca: Cornell University Press, 1978).

The following passage, for example, goes a long way toward making explicit what Wordsworth's autobiographical search for origins is all about:

> The earliest poets of all nations generally wrote from passion excited by real events; they wrote naturally, and as men: feeling powerfully as they did, their language was daring, and figurative. In succeeding times, Poets, and Men ambitious of the fame of Poets, perceiving the influence of such language, and desirous of producing the same effect without being animated by the same passion, set themselves to a mechanical adoption of these figures of speech, and made use of them, sometimes with propriety, but much more frequently applied them to feelings and thoughts with which they had no natural connection whatsoever. A language was thus insensibly produced, differing materially from the real language of men in *any situation*. The Reader or Hearer of this distorted language found himself in a perturbed and unusual state of mind . . . he had no instinctive and infallible perception of the true to make him reject the false . . . the Poet spake to him in the character of a man to be looked up to, a man of genius and authority. Thus, from a variety of other causes, this distorted language was received with admiration; and Poets, it is probable, who had before contented themselves for the most part with misapplying only expressions which at first had been dictated by real passion, carried the abuse still further, and introduced phrases composed apparently in the spirit of the original figurative language of passion, yet altogether of their own invention, and characterized by various degrees of wanton deviation from good sense and Nature . . . This was the great temptation . . . which followed [the first poets]. . . . But the first Poets, as I have said, spake a language which, though unusual, was still the language of men.[9]

This essay on diction actually constitutes a mythical genealogy of the development of poetic language and poetic power. As such, it is Wordsworth's own creative rendering of what amounts to a mythic history of his own craft, a rendering that

9. William Wordsworth, *The Prose Works of William Wordsworth*, ed. W. J. B. Owen and Jane W. Smyser (Oxford: Clarendon, 1974), 1:160–61.

authorizes and valorizes the nature of his own preoccupations as a poet—especially as they are presented in *The Prelude*. Here the transposed structure of a Christian return surfaces as the poet's desire that poets and their poetry return to the privileged language of the "earliest," impassioned poets. Wordsworth's view reflects a Christian pattern of "natural" creation, fall, and redemption: the first poets wrote in a "natural" language that subsequently fell into "distortion," "insensibility," and "mechanicalness"; this fall requires that poetic language be redeemed by a poet like Wordsworth, who wrote in his *Preface* to *Lyrical Ballads* that "The principal object . . . proposed in these Poems was to choose incidents and situations from common life, and to relate or describe them, throughout, as far as was possible in a selection of language really used by men . . . tracing . . . the primary laws of our nature."[10]

The language of "common" life, the poet emphasizes, was chosen because in it "our elementary feelings co-exist in a state of greater simplicity," and "in that condition the passions of men are incorporated with the beautiful and permanent forms of nature." Since "all good poetry is the spontaneous overflow of powerful feelings," the poet chose to "adopt the very language of men . . . figure[s] of speech . . . prompted by passion."[11] By achieving such a poetry, Wordsworth feels he can unite himself with those he deems the "first poets." Thus at *The Prelude*'s "appointed close" Wordsworth writes that he has "faithfully pictured" the "discipline/And consummation of the Poet's mind" (13:263–66), asserting that he can now stand as an "original" poet, a branch on the genealogical tree sketched out in his essay, where "Poets, even as Prophets," stand "each with each/ Connected in a mighty scheme of truth" (12:301–2). As we will see below, this enabling function is an important goal of Wordsworth's poem.

10. Ibid., 123.
11. Ibid., 122, 124; 126; 131.

While Wordsworth's ideas about the origins of poetry are generally informed by various "primitivist" theories current during the eighteenth century, they have their closest analogue in Vico's cyclical view of history.[12] Vico wrote that the "master key" of his *New Science*, whose cyclical theory of history postulated an original age of the Gods, followed by the Age of Heroes, the Age of Men, and a *ricorso* to repeat the cycle, was his "discovery" that "the early gentile people . . . were poets who spoke in poetic characters."[13] Vico's three ages correspond to three languages; an early "mute language of signs," the "poetic language" of "heroic" man, and finally a "human" language worked out by agreement among people (3–4). In Vico's schema the first spoken language was the language of the poets, a language "formed by feelings of passion" in the "imagination" (33, 5). Since these "theological poets" (69) were the first "wise men," Vico posits their "poetic wisdom" as the "first wisdom of the gentile world," a wisdom that "must have begun with a metaphysics not rational and abstract . . . but felt and imagined as that of these first men . . . all robust sense and vigorous imagination" (74). Vico's "first poets" correspond to Wordsworth's "earliest poets," who wrote in the "excitement" of "passion," while Wordsworth's vision of the earliest poets' language falling into the "mechanistic" language of "ornamentation" duplicates the fall of poetic language into the "vulgar," the "rational," and the "abstract" in Vico's.[14] Vico's *ricorso* is implicit, moreover, in Wordsworth's attempt to return to the connected scheme of poets reaching back to the first Prophet-Bards.[15]

12. For a discussion of the background of ideas informing the thought about poetic origins during Wordsworth's time, see M. H. Abrams, *The Mirror and The Lamp: Romantic Theory and The Critical Tradition* (New York: Norton, 1958), 78–84.

13. Giambattista Vico, *New Science* (Abridged translation of the third edition), trans. Thomas G. Bergin and Max H. Fisch (Ithaca: Cornell University Press, 1970), 5. All further page references to this work appear in the text.

14. See *New Science*, 3–8.

15. See *The Prelude*, 12:298–312.

Wordsworth's hope of achieving a Vichian return to the sources of an "original" poetic language is echoed by the cyclical growth of his mind depicted in *The Prelude*. That is, the historical *ricorso* that Wordsworth seeks for poetry is duplicated by the personal *ricorso* outlined in *The Prelude*'s structure, which depicts a boy's "original," "natural" power, his loss of that power in the growing rationality of his manhood, and his return to the original sources of his power in the reanimation of a proper poetic language. The young poet who is to "redeem" the work of the "earliest poets" must himself first experience the askesis of his own *ricorso*.

This is why, in looking back over the course of his development as a poet, Wordsworth sees a cyclical pattern in the flux of his past experience. He presents his earliest relationship to language as a "natural" one that must somehow be recaptured. That relationship came to the poet in moments when, he writes:

> I would stand,
> Beneath some rock, listening to sounds that are
> The ghostly language of the ancient earth,
> Or make their dim abode in distant winds.
> Thence did I drink the visionary power.
>   [2:326–30]

By the time the young Wordsworth reached Cambridge, the stark contrast between college and rural life made him realize that "I was not for that hour,/Nor for that place" (3:80–81). Writing that he was a "chosen Son" who had come to Cambridge with "holy powers," the poet asserts that since he could "apprehend all passions" (3:81–85) he "was ascending . . . To . . . community with highest truth" (119–20). Because of his "powers and habits" (106) of mind "all/That [he] beheld respired with inward meaning" (129). In these lines, he likens his "steady moods of thoughtfulness, matur'd/To inspiration" (149) to the prophetic, visionary powers of "Poets in old time, and higher up/By the first men, earth's first inhabitants" (152–153). In

retrospect, Wordsworth writes that this point in his development was an "eminence," the "glory" of his youth; a time, in
short, when he had the "Genius" and "Power" to "create" like
"Divinity itself" (169–72).

After depicting the growth of his mind to this "eminence,"
however, Wordsworth recounts the beginnings of a poetic crisis,
one in which his privileged relationship to nature's "language"
began to falter. He writes that he was "misled" by "words," by
"the trade in classic niceties," and the "dangerous craft of picking
phrases out/From languages that want the living voice" (6:124–
31). Later, when the poet was "prompted" by "plain imagination" to write, he recalls that the "visible shape" of his work was
influenced not by "nature's inner self" but by "works of art" and
"the images of books"—a "wilfulness of fancy and conceit"
(8:511–21). In Book 11, "Imagination, How Impaired and Restored," Wordsworth speaks of his "crisis" as one brought on by
his attraction to "reason" and "logic," a crisis that had created
such a "gulph" between himself and the great poets that he
"could no more/Trust the elevation which had made me one/
With the great Family that here and there/Is scatter'd through
the abyss of ages past" (61–63). He writes that he was "cut off
. . . /From all the sources of [his] former strength" by the
influence of "syllogistic words" and by the "Charm of Logic,"
that he had lost touch with the "mysteries of passion" that made
"One brotherhood . . . /Of poets": theirs was for him an "empire
pass'd away" (82–95).

The poem is, of course, written to reach its cyclical climax
in Wordsworth's return to his "former strength," a strength
inherent in his renewed relationship with "Nature's presence."
Concerning the "impairment" of his imaginative powers, the
poet writes near the end of Book 11 that:

> I had felt
> Too forcibly, too early in my life,
> Visitings of imaginative power
> For this to last: I shook the habit off

> Entirely and for ever, and again
> In Nature's presence stood, as I stand now,
> A sensitive, and a creative soul.
>
> [251–57]

The strategy of the poem is embodied in this cyclical structure. Wordsworth seeks to return to the "imaginative power" of the "earliest" poets by returning in his poem to the "sources" of his own poetic power in "early life." To redeem the work of the "first" poets, he must "enshrine the spirit" of his own past "For future restoration" (11:342–43):

> From . . . remembrances, and from the power
> They left behind . . . feeling comes in aid
> Of feeling . . .
> . . . if but once we have been strong.
>
> [11:325–28]

The cyclical pattern inherent in this restorative return to "Nature's presence," it must be noted, does not depend upon the poet's ability to somehow actually return to the places where his lost poetic power was first experienced.[16] It ostensibly depends, rather, on memory. Wordsworth's "renewal," as it is de-

---

16. This is made clear in "Lines Composed a Few Miles Above Tintern Abbey." Although the occasion of the poem is Wordsworth's return visit to a vista above the abbey, the poem is about both the sustenance his memory of it gives him when *away* from it and the *different* way his mind's eye looks on the abbey, compared to his youthful visits to it. Thus, in his absence from the abbey its "beauteous forms" have "oft, in lonely rooms, and 'mid the din/Of towns and cities" given him "sensations sweet,/Felt in the blood, and felt along the heart;/And passing even into my purer mind,/With tranquil restoration" (23–30). This restoration, he observes, comes from feelings of "unremembered pleasure" (31), however, and he insists later in the poem that "I have learned/To look on nature, not as in the hour/Of thoughtless youth; but hearing often-times/The still, sad music of humanity" (88–91). Memory here triggers not something "remembered," but something newly created. In fact, the "presence" that "disturbs" him with "joy" here is not a presence that inhabits nature but one "far more deeply interfused,/Whose dwelling is the/. . . mind of man" (94–99).

picted in his poem, does not come in his actual return to nature
to experience again its visitations of power, but in his creative
remembering of those experiences as they lay scattered in the
disorder of time. For Wordsworth, the restorative power of
remembering is actually rooted in a providential *forgetting* of
what he experienced, and felt, in the past. For from the memory
of nature's visitations the poet "retains" only an "obscure sense/
Of possible sublimity," since the mind remembers only "how
she felt, but what she felt" she remembers "not" (2:335-37).
Remembering the "past" thus becomes a process attended by,
and at one with, poetic creation. Seeking restoration from his
past, the poet inevitably faces its absence, and with that absence, he faces the gulf between his past and his present selves:

> [S]o wide appears
> The vacancy between me and those days,
> Which yet have such self-presence in my mind
> That, sometimes, when I think of it, I seem
> Two consciousnesses, conscious of myself
> And of some other Being.
> [2:28-33]

"Those days" have "self-presence" only because the poet can
fill the "vacancy" between them and himself with a poetry that
seeks to recast them as a paradise of poetic power. Since "feeling
comes in aid/Of feeling *if* but once we *have been* strong," the
poet must postulate this paradise in his poem in order to "remember" it. Since a central characteristic of nature's early visitations is that they are forgotten, memory becomes for the poet
writing his autobiographical poem a providential remembering
of something that is actually lost. The relationship between
Wordsworth and nature chronicled in the first two books of *The
Prelude* describes the "ministry" of nature as an "unconscious
intercourse" between a "Child" and "eternal Beauty" (1:589-90):
the poet writes that his mind was "impregnated," "impress'd,"
and "elevated," by "obscure feelings" that "were forgotten"

(1:614–35). What "Nature spake to me," he writes, was "doom'd to sleep/Until maturer seasons call'd them forth" (1:615, 622–23). The poet writes that he conceives of what nature "spoke" to him in its visitations only as "rememberable things" (1:616).

When Wordsworth circles back in his poem to the restoration of his poetic powers that followed the "impairment" of his imagination, declaring that he stands "Once more in Nature's presence, thus restored," (11:393–94) he does not, significantly, recount the "story" of this restoration, since, in fact, it exists in no single story. Instead, he remembers a series of experiences—past visitations of nature's power—out of their chronological order, all of which *pre-date* the crisis outlined in Book 11.[17] In the final three books of the poem, restoration is not situated in any identifiable past event but is in fact generated in the very moments of the poem's composition. Only after he recollects his famous "spots of time," his experiences on the Plain of Sarum, and his ascension of Mt. Snowden into the narrative that constitutes the final three books of *The Prelude*, can the poet declare himself "restored" (13:262–71). Since restoration attends the activity of remembering what has been lost, its achievement in the poem can only present itself as coincident with this remembering, coincident, that is, with its writing: the experiences of remembering depicted *in* the story of the poem form a series of moments that must necessarily extend into the very activity of its writing. Even in the earlier books, "restoration" is represented as a repeated experience, which in the poem becomes diffused into the very texture of the poet's existence. *The Prelude* begins, for example, with Wordsworth singing the "praises" of the restorative feelings he

17. See, for example, Wordsworth's presentation of his experiences on the Plain of Sarum near the end of Book 12, or the story of his ascent of Mount Snowden which begins Book 13. From passages like these, it becomes abundantly clear that "restoration" did not just come to the poet in a "past" part of his life, but attended the activity of remembering and representing the "past" in the present.

experienced while returning from London to Racedown in 1795, which he conflates with similar feelings attending his return to Grasmere in 1799, after having spent time with Coleridge. However, in Book 4 the poet writes that "restoration came" in 1788 when during his summer vacation he "convers'd . . . with God-like power" (146–56). Again, in 1804, while *composing* Book 7, Wordsworth writes that his "strength" had been "stopp'd for years," and that he "resume[s] with chearful hope" the "Poet's task" because he had been "fit(ted)" with his strength the night before (1–56). By Book 11, though, the poet laments *as he writes* that he is "lost" again (330). This is why he returns to his "spots of time," and why he goes on in the remaining books to "remember" the other visitations with which he concludes his poem.[18]

Wordsworth, then, in seeking to restore his creative powers by returning to his own past to rewrite it, weds the need for a Vichian *ricorso* to what Hegel identified as man's need to "produce himself" in the "practical activity" of art. The poet's "reduplication" of himself in *The Prelude* is enacted in a retro-

18. The ambiguity in *The Prelude* concerning the time of the poet's restoration also surrounds the question of when Wordsworth came actually to feel his "calling" as a poet. Thus, as Raymond Havens has pointed out, "The development of Wordsworth's consciousness [in the poem] that poetry was his 'office upon earth' is by no means clear" (*The Mind of a Poet: A Study of Wordsworth's Thought With Particular Reference to The Prelude* [Baltimore: Johns Hopkins University Press, 1941], 2:552). In Book 3 Wordsworth notes that at Cambridge he felt himself to be a "chosen Son" with "holy powers" (82–83); in Book 4 he speaks of the summer of 1788 as a "dawning" in which, though he "made no vows . . . vows/Were made for me" (341–42); in Book 6 he reiterates that the "Poet's soul" (55) was with him at Cambridge. Yet, according to *The Prelude*, it was not until either 1795, at Racedown, or 1799, when he began the poem in earnest, that he really felt himself to be a poet. In fact, as Havens points out, Wordsworth had written some poetry by 1784 and had begun "The Vale of Esthwaite" and "An Evening Walk" in 1787 (Havens, *The Mind of a Poet*, 553). In *The Prelude*, however, it is not until he has "remembered" his past poetic strength and finished his "History" that he can write that he has "reach'd/The time" when he might "suppose [his] powers" as a poet "confirm'd" (13:266–69).

spective journey whose topography is inward knowledge. The
contents of Wordsworth's art, which are to become "spiritual-
ized" in their "passage" through his mind, are the recollected
contents of his own past.[19] In composing his poem, Wordsworth
hopes that "speaking" of what has passed within him will en-
able him to reenvision his past as the development of Divine
"Genius" and "Power":

> Of Genius, Power,
> Creation and Divinity itself
> I have been speaking, for my theme has been
> What pass'd within me.
>
> [3:171–74]

Since the spiritual value in art, according to Hegel, is produced
in the creative process by the passage of material through the
mind, Wordsworth's ability to transcend his loss of power hinges
upon the mediating power of his own poem and the passage of
his past through it. What "pass'd within" the poet must pass
within him once more in the composition of his autobiographical
poem, so that the process of his "reduplication" in it will help
further the growth of the poet's mind and the restoration of his
imaginative powers. Wordsworth's journey back to wholeness
and poetic power is coincident with the activity of composing
his poem. His narrative seeks to extend his past restoration(s)
in the same way that Augustine's seeks to extend his past conversion—in and by the activity of writing.

Written at the beginning of the Romantic period, though,
Wordsworth's text, as Hartman reminds us, is linked to the
autonomous and individual, so that in the end it becomes "as

19. That is, the incidents of Wordsworth's life are given a "spiritual" kind
of significance (the poet believes) in their passage through his mind. This is
what Hegel calls the "baptism of the spiritual": "A human interest, the spiritual
value which attaches to an incident, to an individual character, to an action
in its plot and in its denouement, is apprehended in the work of art, and
exhibited more purely and transparently than is possible on the soil of common
unartistic reality" (*On Art, Religion, Philosophy,* 55–56).

problematic as the individual himself." Though he is "a pilgrim
gone/In quest of highest truth," in writing his poem he has had
to "travel in . . . dim uncertain ways" (11:391–93). This dimness
and uncertainty specify the kind of "places" where his power
resides. The poet's journey is seen to take place in the half-
light of his own inner self:

> The days gone by
> Come back upon me from the dawn almost
> Of life: the hiding-places of my power
> Seem open; I approach, and then they close;
> I see by glimpses now; when age comes on,
> May scarcely see at all, and I would give,
> While yet we may, as far as words can give,
> A substance and a life to what I feel:
>   [11:334–41]

Wordsworth's poem exemplifies the paradox Hartman identifies
as central to Romantic poetry: the entire weight of having to
transcend the purely autonomous and individual must be born
by the poet personally, so that the problem of subjectivity itself
becomes particularly acute in the poem. The "wide vacancy"
between the author of the poem and its subject makes of them
two consciousnesses, and the freedom of poetic creation has for
its other side the abyss of endless figuration. This is why both
the poet and the poem turn in upon themselves. The burden
of overcoming the loss and the absence felt by Wordsworth at
the beginning of *The Prelude* must be shared by both his past
and his poem, since the two merge in a single present—the
time of the poem's composition.

The poem's insistent self-consciousness is a measure of the
tension generated by such a burden. In the middle of Book 2,
Wordsworth interrupts his retrospective story to complain that
it is a

> Hard task to analyse a soul, in which,
> Not only general habits and desires,

> But each most obvious and particular thought,
> Not in a mystical and idle sense,
> But in the words of reason deeply weigh'd,
> Hath no beginning.
>
> [2:232–37]

Here is another aspect of Wordsworth's serious paradox: in the act of composing a poem that seeks to return to the "beginning," he has come to realize that there may in fact be none. The seriousness of this paradox arises in part from Wordsworth's attempt to return to his own beginnings in writing *The Prelude* and at the same time to make his beginning as an original poet. He writes at the poem's conclusion in 1805 that

> . . . we have reach'd
> The time (which was our object from the first)
> When we may, not presumptuously, I hope,
> Suppose my powers so far confirm'd, and such
> My knowledge, as to make me capable
> Of building up a work that should endure.
>
> [13:266–71]

A key component of Wordsworth's "hard task" of self-analysis is his hope that the activity of composing a poem about his past will *prepare* him to become an "original poet" in the sense outlined in the essay on poetic diction. Thus Wordsworth asserts to his friend George Beaumont, "I began [*The Prelude*] because I was unprepared to treat any more arduous subject, and diffident of my own powers."[20]

The surely unintended double meaning of Wordsworth's phrase about "treating" a "subject" in his poem serves to emphasize its similarity to the psychoanalytic process, for the "I" in his poem is being "treated" analytically as certainly as his past is being treated as subject matter. Here we can supplement our earlier discussion of the general relationship between

20. Ernest de Selincourt, ed., *The Early Letters of William and Dorothy Wordsworth (1787–1805)* (Oxford: Clarendon, 1935), 489.

autobiographical self-analysis and the "talking cure" by noting the self-reflexive text's potential function as a tool for the analyst's own analysis of *himself*. Freud insists on the preparatory necessity of self-analysis for the analyst as surely as Wordsworth insists on it for the poet. Referring to the analyst as someone who must learn to "practice a particular art," Freud asks rhetorically in "Analysis Terminable and Interminable," "But where and how is the poor wretch to acquire the ideal qualifications which he will need in his profession? The answer is, in an analysis of himself, with which his preparation for his future activity begins."[21] While the poet/analyst's qualifications are earned in the preparation of his self-analytical poem, the poem shares the problematic experienced by the analyst: the interminability of analysis (which Freud viewed as at best a mixed blessing). Wordsworth's composition of *The Prelude* was, as we shall see below, a literally interminable experience. Composing it represented an arduous spiritual journey comparable with Augustine's. At the same time, however, it stands as a text exemplary of the serious paradoxes inherent in literary self-representation from the Romantic period on.

The Composition of *The Prelude*

The Prelude's composition was both long and arduous, so it is not surprising that Wordsworth often refers to the process of its writing as a journey. He writes that in composing his poem he has become a "traveller" (3:196), a "pilgrim" (11:392) on a "road" (1:668) who "tread[s] . . . holy ground" (12:251). His poem is a "course" (13:365) and a "path" (2:287) over which he makes "progress" (5:11). This progress, as far as we can tell, began in Goslar in October 1798, when Wordsworth wrote the first passage of what later became a poem intended as an auto-

21. Sigmund Freud, "Analysis Terminable and Interminable," in *The Standard Edition of the Complete Psychological Works of Sigmund Freud*, trans. James Strachey (London: Hogarth, 1964), 23:247–48.

biographical preface to his projected long poem, *The Recluse*.[22]
Over the years, as Ernest De Selincourt has observed, it grew
"to a length [Wordsworth] had not forseen," becoming in time
an "independent" poem.[23]

The stages of this growth roughly parallel the three major
manuscript versions of the poem. The "Two-Part" *Prelude*, written in 1798 and 1799, consists of material that later became (for
the most part) Books 1 and 2 of the 1805 and 1850 versions.
Since the poet did not resume extensive work on the poem
again until 1804, some critics, including its most recent editor,
Stephen Parrish, have conjectured that the "Two-Part" was
intended as a "separate," "finished" poem, to be distinguished
from later versions.[24] This assumption is at best questionable.
Many of the fragments from the poet's Alfoxden notebooks
(1797–98) have the autobiographical texture of *The Prelude* and,
as "Tintern Abbey" (1798) attests, Wordsworth was disposed toward *Prelude*-like verse in the composition of poetry that did
not find its way into his long poem.[25] The abrupt beginning of
the "Two-Part"—"Was it for this . . . "—suggests less a "finished" poem than an autobiographical fragment intended to
eventually be used after a longer passage building up to it, as
it is in fact used in the final longer versions of the poem.[26]

22. For an extensive discussion of these early passages and of the poem's
early evolution, see Stephen Parrish, ed., *The Prelude, 1798–1799 by William
Wordsworth* (Ithaca: Cornell University Press, 1977). See also Mark L. Reed,
Wordsworth: The Chronology of the Middle Years, 1800–1815 (Cambridge:
Harvard University Press, 1975) for a chronology of the poem's composition—
especially pp. 628–55.

23. Ernest de Selincourt, *The Prelude, or Growth of a Poet's Mind, by
William Wordsworth (Text of 1805)* (London: Oxford University Press, 1933),
p. x.

24. Parrish, ed., *The Prelude*, 1798–1799, p. viii.

25. For texts of the Alfoxden Notebooks, see Ernest de Selincourt, ed.,
The Poetical Works of William Wordsworth (Oxford: Clarendon, 1949), 5:340–
47.

26. For a discussion of what Wordsworth may have intended to come before
the "Was it for this" fragment, see Parrish's Introduction to *The Prelude, 1798–
1799*.

Whether Wordsworth thought of the "Two Part" as a finished poem is a moot question, since he resumed extensive work on it in 1804, lengthening the poem to include not only an account of the "ministry of nature" experienced in his childhood but also the story of his life as a student at Cambridge. With this the poem began to take shape as a more comprehensive view of "the growth of a poet's mind." There is little doubt that early in 1804 Wordsworth looked upon what was now a five-book poem as "complete," since he then wrote to Francis Wrangham that he was "engaged in a Poem on my own earlier life, which will take five parts or books to complete."[27] Along the way, how-ever, Wordsworth continued his expansion of the poem to what eventually became the thirteen book, then the fourteen book, *Prelude.* He evidently realized that he could not recount the growth of his mind as a poet without treating of his experiences in France and London or describing the "impairment" and "res-toration" of his imagination. Thus at the end of Book 5 we encounter the following lines:

> Thus far a scanty record is deduced
> Of what I owe to Books in early life;
> Their later influence yet remains untold;
> But as this work was taking in my thoughts
> Proportions that seem'd larger than had first
> Been meditated, I was indisposed
> To any further progress at a time
> When these acknowledgements were left unpaid.
> [630–37]

These various stops and starts in the poem's progress, and the poet's changing sense of its scope and length, parallel long periods—described in the poem—during which the "stream" of his imagination was "stopp'd." Writing at the beginning of Book 7 about his composition of the "glad preamble" which opens the poem, Wordsworth says that this verse represents a "short-liv'd

27. De Selincourt, ed., *Early Letters*, 355.

uproar" and that while it "'twas not long/Ere the interrrupted stream broke forth once more," it flowed "awhile . . . then stopp'd for years;/Not heard again until a little space/Before last primrose-time" (1–13).[28] Likewise, Book 9 begins with a passage that refers both to Wordsworth's "fears" about moving on to a discussion of his experiences in France and, in a more general way, to the experience of writing the entire poem:

> As oftentimes a River, it might seem,
> Yielding in part to old remembrances,
> Part sway'd by fear to tread an onward road
> That leads direct to the devouring sea
> Turns, and will measure back his course, far back,
> Towards the very regions which he cross'd
> In his first outset; so have we long time
> Made motions retrograde, in like pursuit
> Detain'd. But now we start afresh; I feel
> An impulse to precipitate my Verse.
> Fair greetings to this shapeless eagerness,
> When'er it comes, needful in work so long,
> Thrice needful to the argument which now
> Awaits us; Oh! how much unlike the past!
> One which though bright the promise, will be found
> Ere far we shall advance, ungenial, hard
> To Treat of, and forbidding in itself.
>
> [1–17]

The poet's journey through his poem, represented here by the meandering river, is characteristically controlled both by "fear," and by a "shapeless eagerness:" trying to move ahead with his poem, the poet is continually "detained" by the impulse to "measure back his course." His "eagerness" to get on with his long work is an eagerness both to finish the chronology of his life *in* the poem and to get on with the work to follow, the

28. Wordsworth writes here that it was five (changed in the 1850 version to six) years since he composed the "glad preamble." As commentators have often pointed out, the poet is here confusing the date of his escape from the "City" with the date he began to write his poem. See, for instance, Stephen Gill, *The Prelude (1805)*, 246. "Last primrose-time" likely refers to spring 1804 when Coleridge's departure spurred him on to try and complete his poem.

much more grandly conceived *Recluse*. But the same process
of detainment, deferment, and repetition that interminably extended *The Prelude*'s composition also impeded Wordsworth's
ability ever to complete *The Recluse*. Here are this thoughts on
"finishing" his poem:

> I finished my poem about a fortnight ago. I had looked forward
> to the day as a most happy one . . . but it was not a happy day
> for me; I was dejected on many accounts; when I looked back
> upon the performance it seemed to have a dead weight about it,
> the reality so far short of the expectation . . . the doubt whether
> I should ever live to write *The Recluse*, and the sense which I
> had of this poem being so far below what I seemed capable of
> executing, depressed me much.[29]

Wordsworth's dissatisfaction with *The Prelude* was strong
enough to keep him at work revising it on and off until his
death in 1850. It is clear in comparing the 1805 and 1850 versions of the poem that Wordsworth used this time to amend
and alter the earlier version, excising from it aspects of his early
development and state of mind that he later found to be in
conflict with the Christian dogma he embraced as an older
man.[30] The changes Wordsworth made were significant enough
to lead Helen Darbishire to observe that the 1850 version is a
"gloss," a "later interpretation," of the earlier poem.[31] When
the poet writes in Book 6 that:

> . . . I have play'd with times,
>
>   .   .   .
>
> And accidents as children do with cards,
> Or as a man, who, when his house is built,

29. De Selincourt, ed., *Early Letters*, 497. Undoubtedly one of the "many
accounts" was the recent untimely death of his brother John.

30. For discussions of these revisions see de Selincourt's introduction to
The Prelude, Helen Darbishire, *The Poet Wordsworth* (Oxford: Clarendon,
1950), 120–43, and John Jones, *The Egotistical Sublime: A History of Wordsworth's Imagination* (London: Chatto and Windus, 1970), 124–32.

31. Darbishire, *The Poet Wordsworth*, 143.

A frame lock'd up in wood and stone, doth still,
In impotence of mind, by his fireside
Rebuild it to his liking.

[299–305]

he aptly describes his tendency to frame and reframe episodes
from his past as he composes and re-composes his poem, interminably editing it "to his liking."

Critics have noted that many of Wordsworth's revisions play
down his earlier depiction of nature's "mystical" and mysterious
workings, along with the involuntary nature of the action of his
mind, what Darbishire calls the earlier poem's depiction of "the
primacy and self-sufficiency of feeling."[32] The point here is not
that the earlier version is necessarily more truthful in its rendi-
tion of the actual development and thought of the young poet.
Rather, the differences between the two versions of the poem
show the poet's ongoing use of self-reflexive writing as a means
for reenvisioning, reinterpreting, and recreating his past—however soon or late he begins to write about it. Wordsworth's
self-analysis becomes an interminable exercise precisely because
in its inter-subjectivity, it allows the poet's own historization
of his past to continue to re-present his past indefinitely. However, because of the very opportunities offered by this kind of
self-analysis it can never be properly ended.

There is a sense, too, in which Wordsworth's continued revisions of his poem constitute an activity not at all unlike Freud's
view of *repression* in "Analysis Terminable and Interminable."[33]
In this essay Freud likens the mechanism of repression to the
distortions, interpolations, falsifications, and additions that can
be effected in an original text by the act of revising it. Thus,
Freud writes, if in "later times" a text is found to contain things
that are "undesirable," the act of revision can, by "crossing out,"
replacing old words and sentences with new ones, or by putting
something "which said exactly the opposite" in place of an orig-

32. Ibid., 124.
33. Freud, *Standard Edition*, 23:236.

inal passage, make the original text "innocuous." This kind of revision can so repress what the author had originally said, Freud concludes, that the final text, if it could be compared with its original, would seem in places to be untruthful.

This kind of editing process characterizes the poet's activity at every stage of the poem's framing: Wordsworth "edits" the fragments of his memory in the initial composition of *The Prelude*— a very problematic task, since "The days gone by/Come back upon me from the dawn almost/Of life . . . I approach, and then they close" (11:334–37)—and then again as he sorts and reworks fragments of his poem until it is rebuilt into a revised *textual* chronology.[34] Wordsworth is caught up in this continual rebuilding, as we saw earlier, because the power he seeks really "hath no beginning":

> . . . But who shall parcel out
> The intellect, by geometric rules,
> Split, like a province, into round and square?
> Who knows the individual hour in which
> His habits were first sown . . .
>   [2:208–12]

Lacking knowledge of this "individual hour" and understanding that his poetic power really has no identifiable "beginning," the poet who seeks to recapture that power by writing his autobiographical poem must "parcel out," must "edit," the dim, uncertain, and fragmented details of his own past. The finality promised by the return to origins is thus displaced by the unending process of having always to begin again and again.[35] This

34. Perhaps the primary example of this is Wordsworth's placing of the "spots of time" passage in Book 11. It appeared originally in Part One of the "Two-Part" *Prelude* as part of Wordsworth's recounting of his childhood. In the longer poem it has a much different function, appearing in a Book not about the early "ministry" of nature but the much later "impairment" and "restoration" of the mature poet's imagination.

35. For an extended discussion of "beginning" in nineteenth- and twentieth-century literature, especially as distinguished from the concept of "originating," see Edward W. Said, *Beginnings: Intention and Method* (Baltimore: Johns Hopkins University Press, 1975).

process, made explicit in the stops and starts and revisions of the poem's composition, turned the continuous writing of *The Prelude* into an Eliotic task of shoring fragments against the poet's own ruin.

Editing and representing the past in the initial composition of his poem, and then reviewing and re-sorting this first representation into another "frame," Wordsworth links visionary and scriptive revision in a single dialectical movement that subordinates remembering to continually "playing with time." The editorial nature of this enterprise is implicit in Wordsworth's vision of himself as the "curator" of a museum:

> . . . roving as through a Cabinet
> Or wide Museum . . .
> . . . where little can be seen
> Well understood, or naturally endear'd
> Yet still does every step bring something forth
> That quickens, pleases, stings; here and there
> A casual rarity is singled out,
> And has its brief perusal, then gives way
> To others, all supplanted in their turn.
>
>   .   .   .
>
> The head turns round, and cannot right itself;
> And though an aching and a barren sense
> Of gay confusion still be uppermost,
> With few wise longings and but little love,
> Yet something to the memory sticks at last,
> Whence profit may be drawn in times to come.
>   [3:652–68]

The museum in Wordsworth's simile represents both the present and the past. The roving poet encounters things "singled out," artifacts existing almost by themselves, in a present where "little can be seen" or "understood," where one perception gives way to another in quick succession. It is in this museum—the poet's own mind—that past "artifacts" are "enshrined" to be drawn forth for "profit." The method of the curator, like that of

the editor, is implicit in these "brief perusal[s]," these fragments which each become displaced by another until they are
finally re-collected into the poem's own continuity.[36] Thus, when
Stephen Parrish writes that the poem's initial composition "was
mainly a matter of fitting pieces of verse together, like parts of
a puzzle . . . [by a] process of re-sorting, inserting, and expanding," he is only verifying what the poet tells us in his
poem.[37] In the final analysis, the poem itself is a "wide museum"
full of written fragments, a museum in which the poet has attempted to collect the past from its dismembered state into a
remembered and transfigured pattern.

Seen from this point of view, the "wide . . . vacancy" (2:28–
29) Wordsworth feels between his past and present selves (which
makes him feel like "two consciousnesses") is a beneficent one.
The "self-presence" (2:30) of the past exists only because the
poet has attempted to fill its "vacancy" with a poetry which
seeks to creatively recast it. Like any museum, *The Prelude*
can only represent the past by being discontinuous with it.
While writing the poem was Wordsworth's attempt to provide
a series of epiphanic moments for his life, he could do so only
by *interfering* with his past. He was attempting, he wrote, to
"rescue from decay the old/By timely interference" (1:126–27).
Here the congruity between the poem's story and the goal the
poet had in writing it becomes explicit. For the "decay" his
poem seeks to alleviate is the decay of his own poetic powers.

36. Wordsworth's museum metaphor suggests an archeological relationship
to the past like the one developed by Freud. Freud writes that the analyst's
"work of construction, or, if it is preferred, of reconstruction, resembles to a
great extent an archeologist's excavation of some dwelling-place that has been
destroyed and buried or of some ancient edifice. The two processes are in
fact identical, except that the analyst works under better conditions. . . . [J]ust
as the archeologist builds up the walls of the building from the foundations
that have remained standing . . . so does the analyst proceed when he draws
his inferences from the fragments of memories" ("Construction in Analysis,"
Standard Edition, 23:259).
37. Parrish, ed., *The Prelude, 1798–1799*, 21.

That is, the dramatic crisis that brings the poem to an end, the story of the "impairment" and subsequent "restoration" of Wordsworth's own imagination, parallels the dramatic crisis animating its composition. What he seeks to interfere with, in beginning to write the prelude to his great work as a poet, is his *inability* to do so, for the poem was in part written to justify the future designs he had for *The Recluse*, to show that "in some sort I possess'd/A privilege, and that a work of mine / . . . might become/A power like one of Nature's (12:308–12). It was written, that is, to help "fix" his "wavering" poetic powers in the present:

> [M]y hope has been that I might fetch
> Invigorating thoughts from former years,
> Might fix the wavering balance of my mind,
> And haply meet reproaches, too, whose power
> May spur me on, in manhood now mature,
> To honorable toil.
>
> [1:648–53]

Since, as his sister reminded him, "preserving" himself "A Poet" was contingent upon his maintaining "a saving intercourse / With my true self" (10:914–19), what better way could there be to rescue and preserve his poetic power than in the very activity of composing a self-analytical autobiographical poem about just such a *prior* achievement?

That composing *The Prelude* was to constitute this saving intercourse for Wordsworth is clear enough from what he says about both his state of mind and his needs as a poet in Book 1. In its initial state, as part of the "Two-Part" *Prelude*, Book 1 makes this function explicit; in its revised state (1804), the poem's recuperative function is reiterated and highlighted. Writing in 1799 of "that day" (1:57) of which he sings in the "glad preamble" (1:1–54) and which he later used to open his longer version of the poem, Wordsworth speaks of how his "spirit" seemed "singled out . . . for holy services," how on that

day "great hopes" and "assurance[s] of some work/Of glory . . .
forthwith to be begun" were his (59–87).[38] Going on to speak
of what later "ensued," Wordsworth writes that "speedily a
longing in me rose/To brace myself to some determin'd aim"
(123–24). Although commentators long assumed that the "glad
preamble," including the succeeding lines ending at line 141,
referred to Wordsworth's walk from Bristol to Racedown in 1795
and his life there with Dorothy, John Finch has argued convincingly that they refer, rather, to Wordsworth's walk to Grasmere—after parting with Coleridge—in November 1799.[39] While
the first 141 lines seem to conflate the Racedown and Grasmere
periods, the time at Grasmere was one of great hope for the
poet (unlike the Racedown period) and fits better the phrase
"happiness entire" (122) that Wordsworth uses to describe his
"complete composure" during this time.

Exactly where and when Wordsworth felt this "happiness"
and "composure" is less important than his using this state of
mind to establish an opening mood for his poem—though it is
significant that we now know that it refers to a time during
which he was writing the poem, not a time before it. In the
duplicate fair copies of the "Two-Part" *Prelude* (made in 1799),
the poem, as is well known, begins in mid-line with the phrase
"was it for this." There has been much conjecture about what
kind of passage Wordsworth might have intended to use to
open a more finished version of his autobiographical poem.
Parrish argues convincingly that drafts for a preamble to the
poem found in manuscript JJ "were meant to precede the coherent central passage" that begins "was it for this." He argues

38. On this dating see John Finch, "Wordsworth's Two-Handed Engine," in
Bicentenary Wordsworth Studies in Memory of John Alban Finch, ed. Jonathan
Wordsworth (Ithaca: Cornell University Press, 1970), 1–13. For an excellent
discussion of the autobiographical nature of Book 1 and its purpose as it
emerged as such, see David P. Haney, "The Emergence of the Autobiographical Figure in *The Prelude*, Book I" in *Studies in Romanticism*, 20:1
(Spring 1981), 33–63.

39. Finch, "Wordsworth's Two-Handed Engine," passim.

that they are the "only clue" extant that indicates what Wordsworth originally intended for his poem's opening. Since these fragments speak of the "rushing power" of both nature and the "mind," Parrish concludes that the "this" of the "Two-Part's" opening line "seems . . . to have been the powerful disturbance of mind occasioned by a superabundant flow of inspiration."[40]

Now this is particularly interesting because Wordsworth composed the present lines 55–271 when he returned to his poem early in 1804, using them after the "glad preamble" to make the "this" refer to his inability to write *The Recluse*. Thus, as Parrish observes, when Wordsworth returned to his poem his mood was "altered" from what it had been when he wrote the "glad preamble," for his "hopes of carrying out some high poetic ambition had become stalled."[41] Lines 55–271 chart a falling off from the "happiness" of 1799, establishing the longer poem's opening mood of discouragement and poetic impairment. This is made explicit at line 134 when Wordsworth slips almost inadvertently from talking about his discouragement in

40. For Parrish's speculations on this matter, see *The Prelude, 1798–1799*, 3–6, 123–24.

41. Ibid., 36. Wordsworth writes here that "When, as becomes a man who would prepare/For . . . a glorious work, I through myself/Make rigorous inquisition, the report/Is often chearing" (157–59). He has, he reports, the poet's "vital soul," a sense of "general truths," and a store of "Forms" and "images," all of which are necessary to "build up a Poet's praise" (160–68). What he lacks, though, is a "theme"; specifically, "names" and events from the past that he might "summon back from lonesome banishment" to "make them inmates in the hearts of men/Now living" (169–76). After rehearsing a variety of possible "themes"—a "British theme," "some old/Romantic tale, by Milton left unsung," stories from Plutarch and Gibbon, tales of the "first Conquerors of the Indian Isles," of Gustavus or Wallace—the poet laments, finally, that "deadening admonitions" make him feel that this "whole beauteous Fabric seems to lack/ Foundation . . . appears throughout/Shadowy and unsubstantial" (177–228). Though he "yearns[s] towards some philosophic Song" (230) he writes that he now lives "from day to day . . . a mockery of the brotherhood" of poets, "with no skill to part/Vague longing . . . From paramount impulse . . . Humility and modest awe themselves/Betray me, serving often for a cloak/To a more subtle selfishness, that now/Doth lock my functions up in blank reserve" (238–48).

the past to talking about it in the present. He writes that "I
have been discouraged" (134), that wherever his mind "turns
she finds/Impediments from day to day renew'd" (140–141).

This, then, was the poet's state of mind when he returned to
his poem, and greatly expanded it, in 1804. The restoration
he hoped for through the activity of composition in 1799, when
he wrote that he wanted to "fetch" his "former" poetic "power,"
is sought again in 1804 when he writes a new end for Book 1:

> One end hereby at least hath been attain'd,
> My mind hath been revived, and if this mood
> Desert me not, I will forthwith bring down,
> Through later years, the story of my life.
> The road lies plain before me; 'tis a theme
> Single and of determined bounds; and hence
> I chuse it rather at this time, than work
> Of ampler or more varied argument.
>
> [664–71]

This passage emphasizes the relationship Wordsworth keenly
felt between working on his autobiographical poem and working
through the problems he encountered in his development as a
poet. We have already seen that during the journey of the
poem's composition, the mood of this revival deserted him
many times. As the size and scope of *The Prelude* increased,
its "Single and . . . determined bounds" multiplied and expanded: the "Two-Part" *Prelude*'s overriding preoccupation with
a boy's "ministry" under nature's hand became a five book
poem expanded to include his college years, which in turn
became the 1805 and 1850 versions, which chronicled the impairment and restoration of the poet's imagination—an impairment paralleled by the one which led to the poem's composition
in the first place. There is, then, an intimate link between
the changing length and scope of Wordsworth's poem and the
"growth" of his mind. One aspect of the poet's preoccupation
with returning to his past to be "nourished" and "repaired" is

his constant returning to his own past manuscripts, to be nourished again by repairing and expanding them. While *The Prelude* is only the lengthiest example of Wordsworth's tendency to write about the restoration he believed to occur in the interaction between past and present, it remains a very special one. For in *The Prelude*, this restoration is sought in the intermixing of past and present poetic fragments, brought together by the Poet-Editor-Analyst in a journey based on the *poetic* articulation of memory.

CHAPTER TWO

Something Evermore About to Be: "Wordsworth" and the Poetics of Revision

In the preceding discussion of *The Prelude*, Hegel's term "practical activity" seemed particularly apt as a description of both the nature and function of Wordsworth's autobiographical art. As practice for writing *The Recluse* and as purposeful self-analysis, the poem's composition was, for Wordsworth, a profoundly practical activity. With the growth of his mind in part dependent upon the growth of his poem and with the search for his own origins tied to his quest to become an original poet, it is no wonder that the poem took its shape less in relation to the past it was chronicling than to the present needs it was seeking to meet. We now need to look more closely at just how these needs determined the practical activity of composition, and at how that composition came insistently to focus on the problem of literary—as well as psychological—subjectivity, and the difficulties inherent in its representation.

Repetition, Recollection, and the Art of Forgetting

In noting the oft-remarked parallels between the recuperative strategies of Wordsworth and Freud, Harold Bloom has observed that "Wordsworth is a crisis-poet, Freud a crisis-analyst; the saving movement in each is backwards into lost time."[1] Having followed Wordsworth's journey towards restoration as it was enacted in his composition of *The Prelude*, we can observe that this "saving movement" applies equally to the quality of Wordsworth's imaginative vision and to the revisionary quality of his writing. That is, there is a functional link between his preoccupation with returning in memory to his past to be "nourished" and "repaired," and his habit of constantly returning to his own past manuscripts to be nourished again by repairing and expanding *them*. The restoration comes from the "nourishment" received in reenvisioning a significant moment in the past. In his most famous explanation of this phenomenon, the "spots of time" passage, Wordsworth writes that when he is "depress'd," his mind can be "nourish'd" and "invisibly repair'd" by remembering a past epiphanic moment (11:258–65). "Not seldom," he writes elsewhere in the poem, "individual remembrances,/By working on the Shapes before my eyes,/Became like vital functions of the soul," impregnating his present thought with "my early feelings" (8:786–92). This "saving movement" back into time is paralleled by the retrospective movement of the poem's writing, which seeks, as we saw, to "invigorate" and "revive," to "fix the wavering balance" of the poet's mind, by recapturing the past in writing and rewriting it. In composing the poem, the mind's search to recover a lost time is paralleled by the poet's need to return to, and repair, the manuscripts which chronicle the search for that recovery.

The "backwards movement" of *The Prelude*, then, is a complex one. In both the substance and execution of the poem,

1. Harold Bloom, "The Internalization of Quest Romance," in *Romanticism and Consciousness: Essays in Criticism*, ed. Harold Bloom (New York: Norton, 1970), 7.

the poet attempts to move *forward* and yet he employs a series of repetitions that continually move him *backward*. Wordsworth's poem in fact depends on both a conscious and unconscious attachment to repetition, and that attachment needs to be understood for the way it both sustains and limits his project. In the first place, the interminableness of Wordsworth's poetic journey is determined in part by a kind of poetics of repetition. In *Beyond The Pleasure Principle*, Freud connects the interminableness of analysis to the compulsion to repeat, a connection which, when it is fully elaborated, helps to suggest why Wordsworth's "restoration" came to depend so heavily upon the process of repetition.[2] In his essay, Freud associates the repetition compulsion with an organism's desire for regeneration, the urge to "restore an earlier state of things."[3] Expanding on this idea in his "New Introductory Lectures" he observes of this urge, "We may suppose that from the moment at which a state of things that has once been attained is upset, an instinct arises to create it afresh and brings about . . . a 'compulsion to repeat.'"[4] We have already seen that *The Prelude* begins out of just the anxiety Freud describes here—the poet's need to "create afresh" a former "state" in which his poetic power will be recaptured. In its attempt to repeat for the poet the initial restoration of his imaginative power, *The Prelude* can be seen to depend compositionally and structurally on repetition.[5]

2. See Freud, "Beyond the Pleasure Principle," *Standard Edition*, vol. 18.
3. Ibid., 57.
4. Freud, *Standard Edition*, 15:106.
5. When Wordsworth writes at the end of Book 11 that he is "restored" (394) he does not, significantly, recount the story of this restoration since, in fact, there is no single story of it. Instead, he "repeats" a series of experiences— *past* "visitations" of nature's power—out of their chronological order, all of which *pre-date* the crisis and restoration outlined in Book 11. See, for example, Wordsworth's presentation of his experiences on the Plain of Sarum near the end of Book 12 (an event which took place in July–August 1793), or the story of his ascent of Mount Snowden which begins Book 13 (an event which took place in summer *1791*). It is only after he recollects (and thus "repeats") these experiences in the chronology of his poem that he can declare himself "restored" (13:262–71).

As many commentators have also noted, Wordsworth's poem tends to repeat many of the same ideas and experiences over and over again.[6] Much of Book 8 ("Retrospect"), for example, repeats material presented earlier in another form, including another description of London, although Book 7 is entirely devoted to his stay there.[7] The compositional history of Wordsworth's poem, as we have seen—characterized by its various versions and the poet's constant revisions of them—is very nearly a case history of the repetition compulsion played out in the scene of writing. Wordsworth, however, was by no means unaware of the importance of repetition in his work, and there is a way in which the technique of his analytical poem already understands Freud. The past, Wordsworth writes, has curative potential, and becomes "habitually dear" to him by becoming "allied" to his "affections" (1:638–39) with

> . . . the impressive discipline of fear,
> By pleasure and repeated happiness,
> So frequently repeated . . .
> [1:631–33]

On the other hand, Wordsworth was well aware that this desire to repeat frequently also could have an adverse effect on his poem: "If, when the work shall be finished, it appears to the judicious to have redundancies, they shall be lopped off, if possible; but this is very difficult to do, when a man has written

6. See for example Herbert Lindenberger, *On Wordsworth's Prelude* (Princeton: Princeton University Press, 1963), who writes that *The Prelude* is "saying essentially the same thing again and again," so that there is less "real progression" in the poem than "restatements of the poet's efforts" at overcoming the loss of his power (188), and Raymond Havens, *The Mind of A Poet* (Baltimore: Johns Hopkins University Press, 1941), who notes Wordsworth's "tendency to retrace ground already covered." When he "found he had more to say about a subject," writes Havens, Wordsworth would "give a fresh account of it instead of incorporating the new material with the old" (2:565).

7. See Book 7. Wordsworth explains in Book 8 why he feels the need to write again about London, insisting that his earlier "Verse play'd only with the flowers," that it constituted only a "simple look/Of child-like inquisition" on the part of a poet in a "light mood/Wholly beguiled" (680–87).

with thought; and this defect, whenever I have suspected it or found it to exist in any writings of mine, I have always found incurable. The fault lies too deep, and is in the first conception."⁸ The poem's "first conception"—which we should note here is also called its "deepest fault"—is its attempt to repeat "the spirit of the past/For future restoration" (11:342–43). The "fault" of its "redundancies" lies in part in the poet's unavoidable linking of poetic power with a complex attempt to recapture lost time.

Wordsworth also defends his use of repetition in attempting to articulate what he calls his "deep" thoughts. In a note to "The Thorn," Wordsworth describes his use of repetition in a way congruent with Herbert Lindenberger's observation that in *The Prelude* "Wordsworth is constantly at work finding new ways to invoke the inexpressible."⁹ Wordsworth writes:

> There is a numerous class of readers who imagine that the same words cannot be repeated without tautology: this is a great error. . . . Words, a Poet's words more particularly, ought to be weighted in the balance of feeling, and not measured by the space which they occupy upon paper . . . every man must know that an attempt is rarely made to communicate impassioned feelings without something of an accompanying consciousness of the inadequateness of our own powers, or the deficiencies of language. During such efforts there will be a craving in the mind, and as long as it is unsatisfied the speaker will cling to the same words, or words of the same character . . . repetition and apparent tautology are frequently beauties of the highest kind . . . the mind luxuriates in the repetition of words which appear successfully to communicate its feelings.¹⁰

8. Ernest de Selincourt, *The Early Letters of William and Dorothy Wordsworth (1787–1805)* (Oxford: Clarendon, 1935), 489. Note how Wordsworth insists here that repetition intrudes even when he writes "with thought," implying that such repetitions work their way into his poem regardless of his conscious attempts to suppress them.

9. Herbert Lindenberger, *On Wordsworth's Prelude* (Princeton: Princeton University Press, 1963), 188.

10. *The Prose Works of William Wordsworth*, ed. W. J. B. Owen and Jane W. Smyser (Oxford: Clarendon, 1974), 2:513.

The "craving in the mind" of the poet to "communicate impassioned feelings" must at times be satisfied with repetition because of the "inadequateness" of his powers, and the "deficiencies of language." For Wordsworth there is an important sense in which the seemingly antithetical activities of *repeating* and *imagining* work together in his attempts at restoring his poetic powers by writing *The Prelude*. In his essay on the relation between imagination and repetition in literature, Edward Casey stresses the importance of just such a "conjoint action": "Imagining can concern itself with possibilities which stem from the past, [and] repetition can direct itself into the future, and both acts take place in the present. Furthermore, far from being mutually exclusive, imagination and repetition are capable of conjoint action, combining in projects in which the activities of either one alone would be insufficient."[11] The *Prelude* is just such a project: the activity of its work takes place, of course, in the present, and yet it attempts to repeat "possibilities which stem from the past . . . into the future" by the "conjoint action" of repeating and imagining. As an autobiographical work, *The Prelude* seems by definition to be a kind of repetition. As a poem, though, it is also quite explicitly a work of the imagination. In the double activity of both remembering and imagining his past, the poet's contemporary historization of that past imaginatively reformulates its meaning in a way he hopes will transform the nature of the present it has determined.

On both the aesthetic and psychological levels, then, the poet's creative aspirations in *The Prelude* depend upon the plasticity of the imagination's relationship to the past, rather than on the mind's ability to faithfully re-present a "true" past. This is why Wordsworth can affirm the "confusions" of his head-spinning tour through the museum of his mind as "gay," and why, later in the poem, these same confusions are called "Im-

11. Edward Casey, "Imagination and Repetition in Literature" in *Yale French Studies* 52 (1975), 249.

pediments that make [the poet's] task more sweet" (4:261). From this point of view the inability of the poet's mind, working in a retrospective mode, to separate fact from fiction, to recognize,

> . . . what portion [of memory] is in truth
> The naked recollection of that time,
> And what may rather have been call'd to life
> By after-meditation
>
> [3:645–48]

is hardly a liability. On the contrary, it is at the very center of the restorative hope Wordsworth had for his poem. The imagination's power to "quicken" the self comes to the poet in a "second look" ("look again/And a new quickening shall succeed" [8:728–29]), a "look" which takes the past as its point of departure but which seeks to repeat it transfigured in another pattern.

Wordsworth's imaginative recollection of his past takes place in the moments he writes, but it is an effort which looks to the future. *The Prelude* is thus based on a Kierkegaardian idea of repetition, a forward moving action that Kierkegaard contrasts to the backward movement of recollection itself: "Repetition and recollection are the same movement, only in opposite directions; for what is recollected has been, is repeated backwards, whereas repetition properly so called is recollected forwards".[12] Simple recollection for Kierkegaard implies that "all that is has been," while repetition has the "character of novelty" because it "affirms that existence which has been now becomes."[13] This is precisely the affirmation Wordsworth seeks in his poetic repetition of the past. He saw writing *The Prelude* as an act of becoming, as a self-transformative repetition of his own past. "A mighty mind," Wordsworth writes, "Exerts upon the outward face of things" a "domination" which "moulds them" in "trans-

12. Sören Kierkegaard, *Repetition: An Essay in Experimental Psychology,* trans. Walter Lowrie (Princeton: Princeton University Press, 1941), 3–4.
13. Ibid., 34.

formations" which can "create" an "existence" (13:69–96). Since the "vacancy" between the poet and his past is "so wide" that he cannot say what is a "naked recollection" or an "after meditation," he is able to use the power of the imagination, allied with repetition, to "enshrine the spirit of the past/For future restoration."

The complexity of this attempt led the poet into a paradox which undoubtedly contributed to the poem's unwieldy size and shape, for the success of his ostensibly retrospective poem depended less on his ability to represent the "facts" of his past faithfully than on the ability of his poetic power to shape a "past" appropriate to the purposes of his art. In this way "crisis" and "restoration" came to exist *conceptually*, as well as historically, for Wordsworth. While his movement between the two animates the story of *The Prelude*, it also provides a structure for the poem. Thus "crisis" and "restoration" become narrative events that can be projected forward or backward to fit the *poem's* chronology, and they are connected less to historical "fact" than to the poet's needs as he is writing.

The Prelude's reliance upon repetition is in a way unavoidable, since a significant portion of its power ostensibly comes from retrospection. Paralleling this reliance, of course, is a concomitant preoccupation with "restoration": because the poem, in a fundamental way, begins with the poet's consciousness of *absence*, repetition becomes a tool for restoring "presence"— the word appears again and again in the poem. Much of *The Prelude's* sustaining energy, then, comes from the poet's efforts to represent in language the visionary "Presence" he has lost, but it is nearly always its felt absence that his language affirms. Thus even the nature of *what* Wordsworth actually lost has remained enigmatic.[14] As Hartman has shown, Wordsworth's

14. Wordsworth's own assertion near the end of the poem that he stands restored to (and by) "*Nature's* presence" (11:394, my emphasis) suggests that nature is the lost "object" of Wordsworth's search. But while nature's presence provides the poet with a *focus* for articulating his sense of loss, the compli-

numerous attempts in the poem to articulate what it is he is seeking to recover, make present, or take into himself, most often take the form of periphrastic phrases such as "possible sublimity" or "something evermore about to be," phrases which at best trace a "legacy" of what *cannot* be said.[15] As Hartman points out, things are viewed as absent by Wordsworth in his poem "not because they are lost (though they might be) but because their 'trace' is difficult to substantialize as a noun or a name."[16] The closest thing to an absence, or a lost "object," identifiable in the poem is not nature, or the poet's mother, but the ability of language to adequately represent the objects of the poet's longing. While it is language that must reconstitute "Presence" for the poet, it is the very difference between language and this "Divinity" or "Power" that impinges on his project and that makes him question its efficacy. Although in the past, he writes in Book 3, this power "pass'd within me . . . in the main/It lies far hidden from the reach of words" (171–85). Thus Wordsworth later laments:

> Oh! why hath not the mind
> Some element to stamp her image on
> In nature somewhat nearer to her own?
> Why, gifted with such powers to send abroad
> Her spirit, must it lodge in shrines so frail?
>   [5:44–48]

---

cated character of that search, and its roots in the need to restore *poetic* power, belie the adequacy of this simple designation. Richard Onorato, in his psychoanalytic study of *The Prelude*, argues that the "loss" Wordsworth is seeking to overcome in his poem has its psychological roots in the poet's early loss of his mother, an argument I find interesting, but much too reductive, since both the poem and its poet's preoccupation with loss have origins much too subtle and diffuse to be gathered under so small an umbrella. See Richard Onorato, *The Character of the Poet: Wordsworth in the Prelude* (Princeton: Princeton University Press, 1971), especially Chap. 5.

15. Geoffrey Hartman, "A Touching Compulsion: Wordsworth and the Problem of Literary Representation," in *The Georgia Review* 31:2 (Summer 1977), 359.

16. Ibid.

Hampered by the frailty of language, Wordsworth's poem becomes caught up in the same problematic as Augustine's *Confessions*; both writers confront language's circumscribed ability to convey a "true" image of their own subjectivity, but here, there is for the subject no leap out of language. Wordsworth's consciousness of this serious paradox is so pervasive that the language of his poem (as Hartman shows) at times founders on it. Moreover, the paradox had an impact on the very structure of his poem. *The Prelude*'s insistent self-consciousness, registered in the poet's regular asides about the difficulty of his task, breaks up the purely narrative structure of its form, so that its retrospective story is continually superseded in importance by the problems its subject experiences as he seeks to represent himself. Subjectivity—in both its psychological and discursive forms—is experienced by Wordsworth as a problem that at once disturbs and shapes the form of his work.

We can now see that Bloom's description of the "saving movement" of Wordsworth's poetry as "backwards" inadequately captures the full scope of the poet's inner journey. For the movement both of his thought and of his work, as we have seen, is hardly linear. The past exists for him in the present as the pretext (literally so, after he initially writes it) for an operation of the mind that repeats a *version* of it for the present purpose of helping him to become the poet he once was. There is, for Wordsworth, however, no "where" to go back to. Since his restoration depends on an imaginative repetition of the past, his thoughts are directed inward as well as "backwards," so that his movement is more like a spiral. While the pretext of Wordsworth's poem is that becoming depends on "returning," in actuality it depends upon the visionary and linguistic powers of his imagination as they work in the present moments of writing. It is in these moments that the poem's subject is produced and invented, and the poem's disjointed form is a measure of the difficulty of such a production.

From Blindness to Insight

Having seen the relationship between the history of *The Prelude*'s composition and the analytical function that its writing had for Wordsworth, we are now in a position to observe how the dialectical relationship between vision and revision, on which that function depends, gets written into the very imagery of the poem. To do this we must examine the seemingly paradoxical connection in *The Prelude* between darkness, blindness, and a privileged kind of sight.[17]

We have already noticed that the relationship between memory and insight in the poem is contingent upon a beneficent forgetting that opens the way to a creative (and imaginatively created) second look; and we have observed that Wordsworth's revisionary poetic method is an extension of that process. The crucial preparatory role of *forgetting* in this dialectical process is figured early in the poem as the darkness that precedes nature's visitations. Thus, an important common characteristic of many of the poet's early childhood "visitations" is that they occur at night. During these experiences the young Wordsworth's actual vision is blinded, the mind's eye usurps its perceptive powers, and the subsequent insight takes the form of fantastic images and dreams.[18] A good example of such a se-

17. My use of the terms "blindness" and "insight" will recall de Man's sustained use of them in his *Blindness and Insight: Essays in the Rhetoric of Contemporary Criticism* (New York: Oxford University Press, 1971). Although the reader may (or may not) find some resonance between the operations of blindness and insight described in de Man's book and their operations in Wordsworth's poem, I do not mean to suggest such a resonance. As the following discussion will make clear, images of blindness and the insights they can bring are replete in Wordsworth's poem, and they form a kind of symbolic network that can (and has) been identified quite independently of de Man's theory.

18. For a thorough discussion of these visitations in *The Prelude* and the dialectical relationship between blindness and illumination they help to establish in it, see Geoffrey Hartman, *Wordsworth's Poetry: 1787–1814* (New Haven: Yale University Press, 1964), Chap. 2, and pp. 163–259.

quence is the famous "Boat Stealing" scene in Book 1. Here the young Wordsworth's vision of a "huge Cliff" becomes the "spectacle" of a "voluntary power instinct," a spectacle which drove him frightened from the lake while producing a "darkness" in his thoughts, so that for many days his mind was filled "with no familiar shapes . . . but huge and mighty Forms" that became "the trouble of [his] dreams" (1:372–427).

Wordsworth's early preoccupation with darkness and the inner vision it afforded him is also evidenced throughout the fragments in his Alfoxden notebooks. In one particularly significant passage, Wordsworth writes that

> . . . In many a walk
> At evening or by moonlight, or reclined
> At midday upon beds of forest moss,
> Have we to Nature and her impulses
> Of our whole being made free gift, and when
> Our trance had left us, oft have we, by aid
> Of the impressions which it left behind,
> Looked inward on ourselves, and learned, perhaps,
> Something of what we are.[19]

Here it is "the impressions . . . left *behind*" from a darkness-induced "trance" that lead the poet to insights about himself. Moreover, the poet's insight here is not congruent with the trance—the experience—but comes later, in remembering it. Knowledge does not come in the existential moment but in the retrospective one; it is belated, a poetic creation of what might have been. When Wordsworth writes in Book 2 of *The Prelude* how he stood "in starlight nights/Beneath the quiet Heavens . . . listening to sounds that are/The ghostly language of the ancient earth" while drinking in "visionary power," he insists that his "elevated mood" was "unprofaned" by either "form/Or image" (322–30).

19. *The Poetical Works of William Wordsworth*, ed. Ernest de Selincourt (Oxford: Clarendon, 1949), 5:343–44.

Episodes like this prefigure the cognitive process which will become crucial to the poet of the imagination, whose creative mind will become the "lord and master" of "outward sense" (11:272).[20] The interplay these episodes exhibit between blindness and a kind of insight suggests the *intermediary* role nature will play in the boy's development as a poet (and it belies the simplistic notion that Wordsworth was a "nature poet"). The calm of nature's presence activates his mind, but the mind's vision takes place in a kind of reverie beyond the "natural":

> Oft in those moments such a holy calm
> Did overspread my soul, that I forgot
> That I had bodily eyes, and what I saw
> Appear'd like something in myself, a dream,
> A prospect in my mind.
>
> [2:367–71]

Characteristic of Wordsworth's cherished childhood visitations, this passage insists on a beneficent blindness, a forgetting, which must precede the vision proper, which is "something in myself, a dream." Nature and the natural moment *are* important, but as points of departure.

Darkness here functions in relation to insight as forgetting functions in relation to imaginatively "remembering." The darkening of the visible and the forgetting of the past, that is, are both preludes to the imagination's creative re-envisioning of a "presence" beyond what "the bodily eyes" can see, a presence that can only be present in—and made present by—the poet's own imagination as he writes his poem. The importance of this kind of blinding is strongly reasserted in Book 11 when Wordsworth in part blames the "impairment" of his imagination on the "despotic" and "absolute dominion" of his bodily eyes:

> The state to which I now allude was one
> In which the eye was master of the heart,

20. See also *The Prelude*, 2:322–28, and 4:386–95.

> When that which is in every stage of life
> The most despotic of our senses gain'd
> Such strength in me as often held my mind
> In absolute dominion.
>
> [171–76]

For Wordsworth, the "empire" of sight "lay[s] the inner faculties asleep." In this "thraldom" the "*outward* sense" is "transported" but not the "mind," and in this way the poet's imaginative powers are thwarted (188–98, my emphasis). On the Plain of Sarum the thraldom is overcome in a "reverie" of poetic power that comes only after the poet's *invocation* of darkness:

> I called upon the darkness; and it took,
> A midnight darkness seem'd to come and take
> All objects from my sight.
>
> [12:327–29]

The relationship here between the poet, natural objects, and the vision of his imagination parallels, as we have seen, the relationship between the poet, *his own past*, and his imagination. The forgetting, or blinding, which is figured in the poem by a beneficent darkness, provides the same pretext for the poet's imagination during these experiences as it does during his experience of writing the poem. The activity of composing the poem is repeatedly figured by Wordsworth in just this way: the power in his past resides in "hiding-places" he can only approach by "glimpses" (11:336–38); the road he has travelled in composing his retrospective poem has taken him along "dim uncertain ways" (11:391): the past has been "view'd" only amidst its "obscurities" (12:354–55).

The obscure, dim, and uncertain nature of his remembrances, then, far from being a liability for Wordsworth, provides the very context for many of the central insights he "glimpses" as he writes (even though he feels, and would have us feel, that he has simply "faithfully pictured" his "history"). This is akin to what we earlier noted was Wordsworth's need in writing his poem to "interfere" with his past, and it is reflected in the many

instances in which he breaks in on the narration of his past with
an observation occurring to him while he writes. In these asides,
the poem's dependence on the conjoint action of remembering
and imagining is made explicit.

One of the most revealing of these moments occurs in Book
8 when Wordsworth "willingly return[s]" to London to provide
a revised reading of his experiences there, first depicted in
Book 7. In recounting a story neglected in that book, that of
his entrance into the city, he writes

> . . . Never shall I forget the hour
> The moment rather say when having thridded
> The labyrinth of suburban Villages,
> At length I did unto myself first seem
> To enter the great City.
>   [689–93]

(The question of course arises as to why, if this was a moment
he would never forget, he neglected to recount it in Book 7.)
He goes on to write of this moment,

> A weight of Ages did at once descend
> Upon my heart; no thought embodied, no
> Distinct remembrances; but weight and power,
> Power growing with the weight.
>   [703–706]

The story, being told in the past tense, insists that what happened occurred *then*, in the historical moment. But there is an
interesting interruption at this point:

> . . . [A]las! I feel
> That I am trifling: 'twas a moment's pause.
> All that took place within me, came and went
> As in a moment, *and I only now*
> Remember that it was a thing divine.
>   [706–10, my emphasis]

Re-envisioning this experience during the poem's composition—in a Book which is, in a sense, already a revision of part

of Book 7—a "moment's pause" becomes a "thing divine." The visitation of "weight and power," clearly, comes "only now" as he is writing about it. It is immediately after this realization that Wordsworth writes of the "quickening" that comes with looking "again." Breaking in on the narration of his experiences in London, the poet likens this second-sight glimpse of "power" to the experience of a "traveller" passing into a deep cave with only a torch for light. With his first look, the "Shapes and Forms" the traveller sees "vanish, change, and interchange" until "The scene before him lies in perfect view,/Exposed and lifeless" (711–27). But,

> let him pause awhile, and look again
> And a new quickening shall succeed, at first
> Beginning timidly, then creeping fast
> Through all which he beholds;
>
> [728–31]

Perhaps the most famous counterpart of this intrusion is the well known "imagination apostrophe" that occurs in Book 6 during Wordsworth's recounting of his crossing of the Alps. The story of how disappointed he and his companion were to find that they had only inadvertently crossed the summit is followed by a break in the progress of the narration, during which the poet has the following illumination as he writes:

> Imagination! lifting up itself
> Before the eye and progress of my Song
> Like an unfather'd vapour; here that Power
> In all the might of its endowments, came
> Athwart me; I was lost as in a cloud,
> Halted, without a struggle to break through.
>
> [525–30]

The "progress" of the poem is "halted," "here," as the poet is composing it.[21] His "eye" is blinded as he is writing before an

---

21. For an excellent discussion of this interruption see Hartman, *Wordsworth's Poetry*, 39–48.

imminent insight about the imagination's power, and he is "lost"
in his present "struggle," as he was in the past one about which
he has been writing. Unable to "break through" to continue the
progress of the poem, the poet's anxiety mirrors the lost hikers'
anxiety. The illumination he has is the following one:

> And now recovering, to my Soul I say
> I recognise thy glory; in such strength
> Of usurpation, in such visitings
> Of awful promise, when the light of sense
> Goes out in flashes that have shewn to us
> The invisible world, doth Greatness make abode.
>   [531–36]

Recognition and recovery have come here in a "usurpation"
of the "eye" of his retrospective song by a visiting insight as the
poet is composing his poem. The "light of sense" goes out here
in a "flash" that contains a double message: the first is the
one we have been reviewing—that authentic vision is always
preceded by darkness—and the second chastises the poet for
thinking in the past that the moment on the summit would be
greater than the moments of trying, even if he failed, to reach
that summit:

> Our destiny, our nature, and our home
> Is with infinitude, and only there;
> With hope it is, hope that can never die,
> Effort, and expectation, and desire,
> And something evermore about to be.
>   [538–42]

This insight, in allowing the poem to continue, links the motif
of "crossing"—which informs both the poet's narration of his experience in the Alps and the progress of the poem as a whole—
to the journey motif that we have seen to comprehend both the
progress of the poet's life as it is told in *The Prelude* and the
long task of telling it. For more than anything else, the journey
of the poem's complex composition sought to enact for Words-

worth his own crossing from the darkening of his poetic powers to the eventual restoring of them: "We have traced," he writes at the end of his poem, "from darkness, and the very place of birth/In its blind cavern," the course of a fallen imagination "to light/And open day" (13:165–69). Sustained, on the one hand, by a language and a poetic method that repeats and then revises the poet's past and, on the other, by a mode of vision that draws its recuperative imagery from moments of bodily blindness, *The Prelude*'s singular value to the poet lies in what he imagines he "sees" about his past as he writes it. Blindness, paradoxically, is a handicap that allows the poet to "see," but what he sees in part is the interminably repetitive, and hence limited, nature of the autobiographical act.

This is what Wordsworth glimpses in his encounter in London with a beggar who is *actually* blind. In recounting one of his walks through the city, the poet tells how

>   . . . lost
> Amid the moving pageant, 'twas my chance
> Abruptly to be smitten with the view
> Of a blind Beggar, who, with upright face,
> Stood propp'd against a Wall, upon his Chest
> Wearing a written paper, to explain
> The story of the Man, and who he was.
> My mind did at this spectacle turn round
> As with the might of waters, and it seemed
> To me that in this Label was a type,
> Or emblem, of the utmost that we know,
> Both of ourselves and of the universe;
> And, on the shape of the unmoving man,
> His fixèd face and sightless eyes, I look'd
> As if admonish'd from another world.
>   [7:609–23]

This is one of the strongest and most dramatic self-referential moments in *The Prelude*: "smitten" by an image of himself as the blind Beggar, Wordsworth inscribes his sense of the limits of his autobiographical project in the "emblem" which is the

Beggar's note. The blind man's "Prelude"—"a written paper, to explain/The story of the Man"—admonishes the poet because it signifies "the utmost that we know/Both of ourselves and of the universe," and thus reminds him (as he writes) of the difficulties he has undertaken in composing his own story. While the Beggar's literal blindness links him unmistakably, though of course paradoxically, with the visionary poet, it also reminds Wordsworth of the limited nature of his own self-reflexive project.

Its limitations of course serve less to cut off the project than to interminably extend it. Its subject, linked as it is to the poem's power to restore and sustain him, is destined *with* the poem to remain "something evermore about to be." Subjected to what Paul de Man has called the "revolving door" effect of figuration,[22] the subject of Wordsworth's poem has its hope in "effort," "expectation," and "desire," and yet at the same time is entrapped in the poet's ceaseless compulsion to "play with time," to rebuild the poem and its subject again and again to his own liking. Caught between its dependence on fact and its reliance on the power of imagination, Wordsworth's narrative can be neither wholly factual nor wholly imaginative. The same holds for its subject. The subject of an autobiographical work is by nature supposed to be factual but, as the subject of a poem, it is also already figurative. Since it resides in a literary work whose aim is to "restore" its author and since that restoration depends on the poetic power of the imagination, Wordsworth's subject owes its existence not to Wordsworth's *past* but to his *poetry*. This is why the scene of writing becomes for the poem both locus and theater, a site where the language of imagination struggles with the perception of fact, where neither can alone resolve the poet's dilemmas, and where those dilemmas deepen as history and present purpose fold into each other.

22. Paul de Man, "Autobiography as De-facement," *MLN*, 94:5 (December 1979), 922.

CHAPTER THREE

Carlyle and Nietzsche:
The Subject Retailored

Pity that all Metaphysics had hitherto proved so inexpressibly
unproductive! The secret of Man's Being is still like the Sphinx's
secret: a riddle that he cannot rede.
                                    —Thomas Carlyle, *Sartor Resartus*

   While *The Prelude* seeks to enact the Hegelian notion that
in the practical activity of his art the artist can realize himself,
that by passing his own past experience through his mind he
can "reduplicate" himself, we have seen that the poem is in
fact founded on a serious paradox and that its narrative surface
registers Wordsworth's consciousness of this fact in its self-
referential moments of doubt and hesitation. The *poet's* difficulties in achieving self-consciousness, that is, are mirrored by
the *poem's* self-consciousness about its ability to represent that
achievement. Since the two achievements are really one, both
the compositional history of the poem and its structure become
emblematic of the poet writing it. Moreover, the problematical
experience of the poem's composition mirrors the problematical

nature of its subject; and the extent to which the course of its
narration is disturbed by digressions, doubts, repetitions, and
revisions is a measure of the extent to which its practical activity
of self-representation is to its narrator a kind of "riddle," the
creation of what may be an "unproductive" metaphysics.

Focusing upon this aspect of *The Prelude*, as important as it
is, we risk forgetting the relatively smooth narrative conven-
tionality of much of the poem. As intensely self-reflective as it
is and as radical as it is in both its conceptual scope and its
secularized metaphysics, it was nevertheless written early in
the nineteenth, and not the twentieth, century. The questions it
raises about the nature of the self, about memory, representation, and the role of language in self-consciousness, are evident
in the poem as disruptions, which are incorporated as insights
by the poet as he *continues* to write the narrative of his life.
If there is in *The Prelude* the trace of an emerging modernism,
it exists just so—as a trace. If it questions the efficacy of the
autobiographical enterprise, if it encounters the textual self as
an Other, if it hovers for moments near the brink of a vision
of irony which calls into doubt the conceptions of the self and of
writing that are sustaining it, it does so as it perseveres in the
task the poet has set for himself—to "truthfully" narrate his life
and the growth of his mind.

To find the implications of Wordsworth's doubts in *The Prelude* fully realized in a text, we must turn from his poem to the
much more ambiguously self-reflexive work of Thomas Carlyle,
Sartor Resartus.[1] By the time Carlyle began *Sartor*, narrative
autobiography had already become a literary mode ripe for parody. As Wayne Shumaker has shown, the conventions of narrative autobiography emerged during the seventeenth century
and had become transformed during the eighteenth century

1. Thomas Carlyle, *Sartor Resartus: The Life and Opinions of Herr Teufelsdrockh*, ed. Charles F. Harrold (New York: Odyssey, 1937). All further
references are to this edition and appear in parentheses in the text. The
quotation at the beginning of the chapter is from p. 54.

into a coherent and recognizable literary form.[2] Carlyle takes specific aim at the intellectual autobiography, which was conventionally written, Shumaker says, to describe "the origin of the author's ideas and the genesis of each of his works."[3] While such narrative life-histories flourished in the nineteenth century, Shumaker's history makes it clear that the conventions of the literary form were, as he writes, "virtually shaped" by the last decade of the eighteenth century, and that they had become traditional by Carlyle's time.[4] While Wordsworth's poem is in its way a poetic experiment in this tradition, it remained for Carlyle to launch in *Sartor* a full-scale critique of it.

Sartor Resartus and the Mystification of Autobiography

The whole of Carlyle's book, but especially the mock autobiography of Teufelsdröchkh in Book 2, constitutes a parodic critique of eighteenth-century narrative autobiography. It also makes manifest the kind of latent disorder that insistently disturbs both the structure and the subject of *The Prelude*. Published before (1833), but written after (1830–1831) Wordsworth's poem, *Sartor* is born of the same "serious paradox" that Hartman insists is at the center of the Romantic self-referential enterprise. But unlike Wordsworth's poem, Carlyle's text consciously *becomes* the paradox Wordsworth's autobiographical work gives only glimpses of. With *Sartor*, the autobiographical act as the conscious historicizing of an identifiable and duplicate self is thrown rag-tag into the abysses of irony.

2. See Wayne Shumaker, *English Autobiography: Its Emergence, Materials, and Form* (Berkeley: University of California Press, 1954), 1–30. Concerning the emergence of narrative autobiography, Shumaker writes that "The broad lines of autobiographical development . . . are clear. The conventions that today are taken for granted were emergent in the seventeenth century, gradually took form in the eighteenth, and after the publication of Gibbon's *Memoirs* were virtually shaped" (30). For a similar discussion of the emergence of the traditional autobiographical mode Carlyle is parodying see Pascal, *Design and Truth in Autobiography* (Cambridge: Harvard University Press, 1960), 21–49.

3. Shumaker, *English Autobiography*, 26.

4. Ibid., 30.

Morse Peckham, like Hartman, understands the early nineteenth century as a period in which older "religious tools had
worn out." In his discussion of *Sartor* in *Beyond the Tragic
Vision*, Peckham uses the language and imagery of *Sartor* to
make the same point about subjectivity Hartman does:

> In the nineteenth century it was above all religious tools that
> had worn out, and the rationalist-empiricist tools of the Enlight-
> enment. Now we can penetrate the mystery of the title [*Sartor
> Resartus*—"The Tailor Retailored"]. Man's clothes are symbols.
> In creating those clothes, he is a tailor. But his clothes wear
> out. He must, therefore, retailor himself, make himself new
> clothes. At certain periods in history his most important clothes,
> the ones he sews to symbolize the self, are in rags. Such a period
> was the nineteenth century.[5]

Peckham links Teufelsdrockh's "Clothes Philosophy" to Carlyle's
ideas both about the self and about self-representation (a crucial
linkage, as we shall see in a moment). A central idea underlying
Sartor is that the self, and subjectivity, are made ("tailored"),
that they are humankind's own secular productions. Peckham
sees this idea in *Sartor* as emblematic of similar ideas that were
emerging in the first third of the nineteenth century. He cor-
rectly recognizes *Sartor* as a central document of this period
because it articulates and enacts both the necessary "retailoring"
of "worn-out" notions of the subject and of literary subjectivity.[6]

5. Morse Peckham, *Beyond the Tragic Vision: The Quest for Identity in
the Nineteenth Century* (New York: Braziller, 1962), 184–85.
6. This point is also made by Robert Langbaum in *The Poetry of Experience: The Dramatic Monologue in Modern Literary Tradition* (New York:
Norton, 1963), 13, and by Albert J. LaValley in *Carlyle and the Idea of the
Modern: Studies in Carlyle's Prophetic Literature And Its Relation to Blake,
Nietzsche, Marx, and Others* (New Haven: Yale University Press, 1968), who
writes that *Sartor* "regards" the myth of Christianity and its conception of the
self as "totally outworn." "The source of the new religious myth," he continues,
"is simply the self, and it is this belief which Carlyle has emphasized in
branding Teufelsdrockh's experience as paradigmatic, symbolical myth." The
"pattern" Teufelsdrockh's mind follows "becomes a pattern that one creates out
of the depths of the self rather than a pattern to which one submits oneself"
(84).

Commentators like Peckham have often linked *Sartor* to the tradition of spiritual autobiography from Augustine to Wordsworth. What needs to be emphasized here, however, are not the similarities between *The Prelude* and *Sartor*,[7] but the dissimilarities. We have a clue to the locus of these significant differences in Abrams' observation that while there is a kinship between Wordsworth's and Carlyle's works "*Sartor* is . . . a radical experiment in artistic form; . . . unlike *The Prelude*, whose innovations are unobtrusive and easily overlooked, it is . . . blatantly eccentric."[8] Abrams is right, but he goes on to insist that despite *Sartor*'s being a "serious parody" of autobiography, it "plays with and undercuts the conventions it nonetheless accepts."[9] On the contrary, it seems to me that *Sartor* undercuts the literary conventions of autobiography precisely *because* it does not accept them. The message of *Sartor* is not parodic but ironic: Carlyle does not go to all the trouble of undercutting the conventions of autobiography as a way of accepting them but as a way of calling them into ontological question. Abrams smooths over the break between Carlyle and Wordsworth in order to squeeze *Sartor* into the series of texts he sees as timeless "*circular* pilgrimages."[10] In doing so he must reduce the complex purposes of Carlyle's book to its author's need to return "home" to his "father."[11] He dismisses the significance of the book's disorder and privileges the very convention Carlyle is deconstructing.

The seeming disorder of the biography of Teufelsdrockh is thus structured on the familiar Romantic novel of a a self-formative educational journey, which moves through division, exile, and

7. For discussions of the similarities between *Sartor* and *The Prelude* see Langbaum, *The Poetry of Experience*, 12–19, and M. H. Abrams, *Natural Supernaturalism* (New York: Norton, 1971), 65–70, 129–34, and 308–11.

8. Abrams, *Natural Supernaturalism*, 129.

9. Ibid., 130.

10. Ibid., 309.

11. Ibid.

solitariness toward the goal of a recovered home and restored familial relationship.[12]

The disorder of Book 2, as any reader can attest, is hardly one that only *seems* to exist. Moreover, Carlyle's point in so constructing his book is to disorder our sense of the ordering possibilities of any autobiographical narrative. The disorganized state of both Teufelsdrockh's autobiographical documents and his editor's use of them, as we shall see below, is a structural device that also has an important semantic function: Book 2 cannot affirm the "familiar Romantic model" it parodies precisely because it undoes the conventions of literary representation on which the model is based. The whole point of this mock autobiography is to call into radical question the very possibility of achieving the kind of recovery-through-narrativizing on which Abrams' Romantic model is based.

Much more to the point in understanding the relationship between *The Prelude* and *Sartor Resartus* in the context of nineteenth-century ideas about subjectivity and its literary representation is Albert J. LaValley's insistence that Carlyle "goes beyond Wordsworth, admitting to a certain skepticism, a feeling that the Romantic vision of a Wordsworth is too outmoded."[13] While LaValley observes that both Wordsworth and Carlyle focus on the same two processes—the artist's spiritual journey toward self-awareness and aesthetic power and the process of his concomitant literary representation of that journey—he notes that Wordsworth "fears the dissolution of literary structure" and literary "identity" in his "process poem" more than Carlyle does in *Sartor Resartus*.[14] Wordsworth's fear of such a dissolution kept the structure and content of his poem within fairly conventional narrative bounds. Since, as we have seen in discussing *The Prelude*, the poem at once acknowledges and resists

12. Ibid.
13. LaValley, *Carlyle and the Idea of the Modern*, 106.
14. Ibid.

the kind of dissolution that Carlyle's text both embodies and affirms, there is a way in which its relatively smooth surface represents a disjunction between insight and form. Although it is immensely more "disorganized" than the The Prelude, then, Sartor, as LaValley perceptively observes, "shows a greater blending of form and content" than does Wordsworth's poem.[15] However, since this "blending" is of a "tailored" and "ragged" self with a tailored and ragged text, Sartor looks to be less blended than The Prelude. Thus, comparing the surface appearances of each work generates a kind of paradox. Carlyle's blending of form and content is, as LaValley points out, less "troubled" than Wordsworth's but his ideas demand a form that is more troubled than the surface of The Prelude. As we saw earlier, the seemingly untroubled form of The Prelude covers moments in which it acknowledges, and seeks to assimilate, its doubts. Both works roil the waters of literary self-representation, and both do so because their respective authors have moved toward the same kinds of insights about subjectivity and its literary representation. Sartor, however, especially by virtue of its form, moves much more decisively toward consciously questioning the efficacy and value of literary self-representation than does The Prelude.[16]

Before turning to Sartor itself to observe how it deconstructs what Wordsworth's poem seeks to order, we should note the

15. Ibid., 107.

16. William Spengemann also makes this point in a somewhat different discussion of Sartor in The Forms of Autobiography (New Haven: Yale University Press, 1980). He groups Carlyle's text among those works he calls "poetic" autobiographies, the final form in an evolution from the "historical" through the "philosophical." His categorizing Sartor as a "poetic" autobiography makes apparent how inadequate and overly constricting those categories are. We might wonder why so philosophical a work as Sartor is deemed "poetic" while The Prelude is exclusively "philosophical." The value of his categorizations finally founders on his attempt to confine each work in one category when it would just as logically fit into another. For Spengemann's discussion of Sartor, see pp. 110–18.

controversy among Carlyle's critics about whether the book is somehow *Caryle's* autobiography, and how this controversy reflects the book's efforts to undo its readers' preconceptions about autobiographical forms. Critics have always noticed that, as Spengemann recently put it, "the essential ingredients of Teufelsdrockh's biography are based on Carlyle's life."[17] They have also insisted, however, that, in G. B. Tennyson's words, "we must . . . avoid the all-too-widespread error of confusing . . . Carlyle's own life" with the biography of Teufelsdrockh.[18] The critical dilemma reflected by these two views would please Carlyle immensely, for it neatly transfers the problems in *Sartor* concerning Teufelsdrockh and his relationship to his autobiographical writings to the relationship between Carlyle and his relatively autobiographical book. Book 2 is purposefully autobiographical (Harrold's extensive footnotes in Book 2 become a running commentary on the way in which Carlyle's life is reflected in Teufelsdrockh's), and Carlyle seems thus to invite commentators to notice how, as Peckham puts it, *Sartor* is in part an "imaginative autobiography of Carlyle himself,"[19] and how its "quest for meaning," as LaValley writes, "is really Carlyle's."[20] But the argument about whether *Sartor* is an "autobiography" turns the critic into another form of *Sartor*'s Editor, sifting through the book trying to decide whether it is an autobiographical "hoax". If we replace the words "Teufelsdrockh" and "Professor" in the following quotation from the end of Book 2 with the name "Carlyle," and if we substitute "critic" for

17. Spengemann, *The Forms of Autobiography*, 115.

18. G. B. Tennyson, *Sartor Called Resartus: The Genesis, Structure, and Style of Thomas Carlyle's First Major Work* (Princeton: Princeton University Press, 1965), 189.

19. Peckham, *Beyond the Tragic Vision*, p. 181.

20. LaValley, *Carlyle and the Idea of the Modern*, 92. For another discussion of the autobiographical basis of *Sartor*, see John Clubbe, "Carlyle on *Sartor Resartus*," in *Carlyle Past and Present: A Collection of New Essays*, ed. K. J. Fielding and Rodger L. Tarr (London: Vision Press, 1976), 51–60.

"Editor," it becomes ironically clear that *Sartor* is autobiographically to Carlyle precisely what Teufelsdrockh's autobiographical writings are to Teufelsdrockh:

> Here, indeed . . . must the Editor give utterance to a painful
> suspicion . . . grounded perhaps on trifles, yet confirmed almost
> into certainty by the more and more discernible humouristico-
> satirical tendency of Teufelsdrockh, in whom under-ground hu-
> mours, and intricate sardonic rogueries, wheel within wheel,
> defy all reckoning: a suspicion, in one word, that these Auto-
> biographical Documents are partly a mystification! (202)

Sartor Resartus may, then, contain Carlyle's autobiography but
in a "mystified" form, wheeling in "intricate sardonic rogueries."
The book is an autobiography of Carlyle only as far as Book 2
is an autobiography of Teufelsdrockh, and much of what the
Editor says there about Teufelsdrockh can be said also of Carlyle: what "befalls" him in life may be "embodied" in his text
but it "lies scattered, in dim disastrous details" (120–21; and
note the pun on "lies"); "it ever remains doubtful whether he is
laughing in his sleeve at these Autobiographical times of ours,
or writing from the abundance of his own fond ineptitude" (94).
As a writer of autobiography, then, Teufelsdrockh is clearly
an autobiographical figure for Carlyle. But, *Sartor* ends by
implying that the Editor is actually in London and that he may
in fact *be* Teufelsdrockh. So we are left with one final sardonic
suggestion: that Teufelsdrockh and the Editor are both figures
for the sly autobiographer Carlyle. This supposition is supported
by Carlyle's own note on page 13. Speaking of the Editor, who
is given the name "Oliver Yorke," he says that "With us even
he still communicates in some sort of mask, or muffler; and, we
have reason to think, under a feigned name!" (13)[21] This is prob-

---

21. "Oliver Yorke" was the pseudonym of William Maginn, who at the time
of *Sartor*'s composition was the editor of *Fraser's Magazine*, in which Carlyle's
book was serially published in 1833–1834.

ably the aptest description in *Sartor* of Carlyle himself as the Teufelsdrockhean autobiographer.

With the figure of the autobiographer in *Sartor* identified with its Editor and with the accompanying suggestion that writing autobiographically is in fact an editorial process, we return to an analogy familiar from our discussion of Wordsworth's composition of *The Prelude*. The revisionary poetics we saw underlying Wordsworth's poem—his tendency, that is, to "edit" the fragments of his memory, sorting and re-sorting them into a poetic chronology, "parceling out" his "intellect"—represent the methods of the autobiographer made explicit in Carlyle's figure of the Editor. Carlyle's foregrounding of the editing process in *Sartor* makes manifest what is only latent in Wordsworth's poem. In this, as in the eccentricity of its form, he moves beyond *The Prelude* in undermining the conventions and practices of the self-reflexive work. Both are patchwork texts, but Carlyle insists that *Sartor*'s seams show.

While Wordsworth in composing *The Prelude* strove to provide coherence to both the subject ("Wordsworth") and the form of his poem, Carlyle invokes the editorial process to disorder both *Sartor*'s subjects (Teufelsdrockh/Carlyle) and its form. The fragments from journals, notebooks, and successive drafts of his poem were ordered by Wordsworth into autobiographical and poetic coherence as he labored to write a poem about an ostensibly whole and unfied self, brought "together" in the very process of that ordering. Carlyle's book, however, foregrounds *fragmentation* to call into question the kind of ordering process attempted by Wordsworth. Thus the dramatic declaration that Teufelsdrockh's autobiographical "documents" will make "the whole Philosophy and Philosopher of Clothes . . . stand clear" (77) is undercut by their very form: "in place of this same Autobiography with 'fullest insight' we find—Six considerable *Paper-Bags* carefully sealed, and marked successively, in gilt China-ink, with the symbols of the Six southern Zodiacal Signs" (77–

78).[22] Carlyle sets up his reader to depend on Teufelsdrockh's autobiography and then mocks that trust with the introduction of mere scraps and fragments. It is as if we were presented with an unedited version of *The Prelude*:

> Whole fasciles there are, wherein the Professor . . . is not once named. Then again, amidst what seems to be a Metaphysico-theological Disquistion . . . we shall meet with some quite private, not un-important Biographical fact. On certain sheets stand Dreams, authentic or not, while the circumjacent waking Actions are omitted. Anecdotes, oftenest without date of place or time, fly loosely on separate slips, like Sibylline leaves. Interspersed also are long purely Autobiographical delineations; yet without connection, without recognizable coherence . . . Selection, order, appears to be unknown to the Professor . . . [78][23]

On the one hand, the disorganized, fragmented condition of Teufelsdrockh's autobiographical writings are meant as a sign of the limited value of such information, and this chaos serves Carlyle as his central vehicle for communicating how "inexpressibly unproductive" such self-reflexive writings may be in solving the Sphinx-like riddle of "Man's Being." Thus he has Teufelsdrockh ask rhetorically, "what are your historical Facts;

22. Carlyle continually insists that Teufelsdrockh's autobiography will be the key to understanding his philosophy. "To state the Philosophy of Clothes," he writes, "without the Philosopher, the ideas of Teufelsdrockh without something of his personality, was it not to insure both of entire misapprehension?" (11). Without the autobiographical documents, the editor feels "shut out from all public utterance of these extraordinary Doctrines" (11). And again, the editor laments that "often . . . we have to exclaim: Would to Heaven those . . . Biographical Documents were come! For it seems as if the demonstration [of the philosophy] lay much in the Author's individuality; as if it were not Argument that had taught him, but Experience" (52).

23. Later in the book, these autobiographical documents are described as having a "total want of dates," as being "enigmatic" and "chaotic," containing "fragments of all sorts; scraps of regular Memoir, College-Exercises, Programs, Professional Testimoniums, Milkscores, torn Billets, sometimes to appearance of an amatory cast; all blown together as if by merest chance, henceforth [to] bewilder the sane Historian" (108).

still more your biographical? Wilt thou know a Man . . . by stringing-together beadrolls of what thou namest Facts?" (203) On the other hand, as the Editor observes, the disorganized, rag-tag condition of Teufelsdrockh's writings have a mimetic function: "the actual condition of these Documents . . . is no bad emblem" of Teufelsdrockh himself.

> His so unlimited Wanderings, toilsome enough, are without as-
> signed or perhaps assignable aim; internal Unrest seems his sole
> guidance; he wanders, wanders, as if that curse of the Prophet
> had fallen on him . . . [148]

The equations here are clear enough: Teufelsdrockh's auto-biographical writings "wander" because *he* wanders, they are "without assigned . . . aim" because *he* is, and they have an "internal Unrest" which matches their maker's. The "chaotic nature of these Paper-Bags" (148), then, works at once to undo our expectations about narrative coherence in autobiography *and* our expectations about the coherence of its ostensible subject, Teufelsdrockh. This is why he is made to move through his own text as he moved through the world:

> Foolish were it in us to attempt following him, even from afar
> . . . Hopeless is the obscurity, unspeakable the confusion. He
> glides from country to country, from condition to condition;
> vanishing and re-appearing . . . [if] he settles for a time, and
> forms connexions, be sure he will snap them abruptly asunder.
> [152]

The confusion, rapid changes of condition, and the abrupt snapping of connections characteristic of Teufelsdrockh's "life" are reified in the condition of his autobiographical writings to help make the book's central point about "Man's Being": that *he* himself constructs and produces it—in the words of the "Clothes Philosophy"—out of whole cloth. When Teufelsdrockh describes himself it is with a blend of the book's two central images of such a production—that of editing, and that of tailoring:

> I . . . have thatched myself over with the dead fleeces of sheep,
> the bark of vegetables, the entrails of worms . . . and walk
> abroad a moving Rag-screen, overheaped with shreds and tatters
> . . . Day after day, I must thatch myself anew . . . some film
> of it, frayed away by tear and wear, must be brushed-off into the
> Ashpit . . . till by degrees . . . I, the dust-making, patent
> Rag-grinder, get new material to grind down. [56][24]

The idea here that selfhood is a product of labor, that we continuously "thatch" ourselves together anew out of "shreds" and
"tatters," turns the activities of both the tailor and the editor
into metaphors of being. The question Carlyle begs at the end
of this passage—"Am I a botched mass of tailors' and cobblers'
shreds . . . or a tightly articulated, homogeneous little figure
. . . ?"—makes his point, a point reiterated by the very structure of his book. Written during a period when the (especially
divinely given) homogeneity of both the psychological and the
literary subject were being questioned, *Sartor* represents both
subject *and* autobiographer as "a botched mass of tailors' and
cobblers' shreds" to undermine the notion that the self is a
"homogeneous little figure" that can be "tightly articulated."
Otherwise, why, as *Sartor*'s Editor asks of Teufelsdröckh, "per-
plex these times, profane as they are, with needless obscurity,
by omission and commission?" (185).[25]

24. This passage not only represents the "patched" nature of the self; it also
wonderfully parodies the Romantic "Natural Man."

25. *Sartor* ends with the explicit suggestion that it has revealed that being
is *not* homogeneous, and that the "essence" of man—if indeed there is such
a thing as man's "essence"—is not whole and unchanging but discrete and
ever-changing. This suggestion is made explicit in a series of rhetorical questions that in effect recapitulate the whole book: "Here, then, arises the so
momentous question: Have many British Readers actually arrived with us at
the new promised country; is the Philosophy of Clothes now at last opening
around them? . . . And now does the spiritual, eternal Essence of Man, and of
Mankind, bared of [its] wrappings, begin in any measure to reveal itself?" (267).
The answer Carlyle intends to elicit from the reader he has purposefully con-
fused is of course "no." The tone of this passage comes from a self-assured
mystifier. He continues: "Can many readers discern, as through a glass darkly,

This "obscurity," finally, is a *needful* one. It dissolves an idealized vision of selfhood at the same time as it assimilates it, de-idealized, into what Carlyle calls the "actual": "here, in this poor, miserable, hampered, despicable Actual, wherein thou even now standest, here or nowhere is thy Ideal" (196). Carlyle's Actual, a temporal and secular here and now, is the very locus of selfhood because it is here that the work of producing it is undertaken. "Work it out therefrom," he writes, "the Ideal is in thyself . . . thy Condition is but the stuff thou art to shape . . . Produce! Produce!" (196–97). Here again is Hegel's notion of the artist's self-reflexive "practical activity." The pun in Carlyle's line about shaping and "art" reflects his own idea that in the *work* of his art the artist produces his being—whether "in the authentic lineaments of Fact, or the forged ones of Fiction" (75). Selfhood for Carlyle is not homogeneous, but endlessly produced and so tailor-made.

His insistence upon the constructed, edited, "thatched" nature of subjectivity and the practical role of the artist's creative activities in its production, seems to be an indication of the enabling function that Carlyle's own composition of the book had for him. For as Spengemann has observed about *Sartor*, "the narrative becomes an action, rather than the report of an action."[26] Thus the "action" of writing *Sartor* looks in retrospect to be in part the activity of Carlyle's putting himself together as a writer, and the book seems as pivotal to his career as it is to the changing ideas about literary self-representation to which it was contributing. "With *Sartor*," LaValley observes, "Carlyle's conception of the work of art appears in an entirely new perspective. No longer does he as author confront the works of another author . . . no longer is the reader's attention

---

in huge wavering outlines, some primeval rudiments of Man's Being, what is changeable divided from what is unchangeable?" (267–68). Again, Carlyle elicits a negative answer, and this answer is the very *point* of his book.

26. Spengemann, *Forms of Autobiography*, 115.

directed to some subjective transformation outside the literary work. Instead, Carlyle focuses upon the literary work itself as the process of realization."[27] From this perspective, the autobiographical content of *Sartor* and its concomitant emphasis on the transformational value of literary work become signs of how its composition was integral to the process of Carlyle's "realization" as a writer. This is Carlisle Moore's conclusion in his important essay on the "conversion" scene in Book 2. In discussing Teufelsdrockh's "Spiritual Newbirth, or Baphometic Fire-baptism" along the *"Rue Saint-Thomas de l'Enfer"*—which Carlyle insists "occurred quite literally to myself in Leith Walk"[28]—Moore shows how Carlyle's "gradual" conversion over the years 1822–1830 is "compressed dramatically into the *Rue de l'Enfer* narrative."[29] In doing so, he argues that Carlyle's writing of *Sartor* must be seen as the culminating act of that conversion, that "the achievement of the Everlasting Yea and the writing of *Sartor* were . . . intimately connected."[30]

This linkage seemingly clarifies the similar one in *Sartor* between Teufelsdrockh's crisis and conversion and his turn to the *work* of art. For the description in *Sartor* of the "necessity" for Teufelsdrockh's writing an autobiography—his *Sorrows of Teufelsdrockh*—reflects the same kind of necessity that critics like LaValley and Moore have identified for Carlyle's writing of *Sartor*. Thus Carlyle writes that "Poor Teufelsdrockh" must "write his *Sorrows of Teufelsdrockh*" because, "for your nobler minds, the publishing of some such Work of Art . . . becomes almost a necessity. For what is it properly but an Altercation with the Devil, before you begin honestly Fighting him? . . . Happier is he who . . . can write such matter, since it must

27. LaValley, *Carlyle and the Idea of the Modern*, 90.
28. See *Sartor Resartus*, 166, n. 3. For a careful discussion of this note, and possible omissions in it, see Clubbe, "Carlyle on *Sartor Resartus*," 56–57.
29. Carlisle Moore, "*Sartor Resartus* and the Problem of Carlyle's 'Conversion,'" in *PMLA* 70:4 (September 1955), 679.
30. Ibid., 680.

be written . . . and also survive the writing thereof!" (156–57). It would appear, then, that the composition of *Sartor* represents for Carlyle an enabling activity paralleling Wordsworth's composition of *The Prelude*.

The problem with such a conclusion, of course, is that it forgets the fundamentally ironic nature of Carlyle's book, asserting a conventional function for the book that the book is actually at pains to undermine. While it is important that we identify the extent to which Carlyle builds into *Sartor* the convention of recovery, or conversion, through the practical activity of narrativizing the past, we must also acknowledge that this convention forms yet another thread in an ironic tapestry that implies the *impossibility* of such a recovery. The "humouristico-satirical tendency" of Teufelsdrockh, as we have seen, is animated by Carlyle's similar trait, and the motif of recovery-through-literary-work in his book tends to be neutralized by *Sartor*'s status as a hoax. Since it is as much a convention of *writing* as it is a conventional kind of *experience* that *Sartor* seeks to disorganize, the supposed enabling relationship between Carlyle and his book cannot escape the web of ironies that it has spun.

In the end, then, *Sartor* plunges the self-referential literary subject and the traditional methods of its representation into a condition of irony. It begins by insisting on the crucial importance of Teufelsdrockh's autobiographical documents, only to conclude by undercutting their status as "knowledge." *Sartor* blends autobiography and philosophy, proposing to articulate "the spiritual, eternal Essence of Man" (267), but by its "chaotic," fragmented form it deconstructs that "essence" into a representational impossibility. The Editor's suspicion that Teufelsdrockh's autobiographical writings may actually be "figurative crotchets," a "whimsical . . . *chiaroscuro*" (185) whose facts seem little better than a fiction, represents the book's larger suspicion that the autobiographical enterprise is ontologically inseparable from the fictional one. Moreover, it pulls the philosophical ground from under the conception of "being" as a unified, eternal, spiritually generated essence, replacing it with Carlyle's notion of being as a condition that is shaped and produced—in a very temporal "Actual." *Sartor's* privileging of the Editor and the Tailor (who in the form of the poet "first made Gods for men" [290]) at once reorganizes and problematizes the ground of subjectivity and of self-referential literary representation. *Sartor's* emphasis on production and work, on the temporal nature of subjectivity as something that is personally (and socially) constructed, is at one with its emphasis on the fictional nature of Teufelsdrockh's autobiographical documents. The book thus has the double function of secularizing the ground of selfhood and radically undermining the ground of self-reflexive literary construction.

The effect of *Sartor's* irony is to make the doubts we saw in Wordsworth's *Prelude* explicit enough to dissolve the tenuous line drawn by the poet between factual and fictional self-representation. While *The Prelude's* self-consciousness is a sign of the *seriousness* of Hartman's "serious paradox," *Sartor's* irony and its disordered form are signs of how *serious* Carlyle was about representing that paradox *in* his text. This fundamental difference between the two works is a measure of the philosophical and aesthetic distance between the two writers, a distance that marks the beginning of an evolving set of strategies for self-reflexive representation.

History as Dramatic Narrative

We can better understand the formal innovations in autobiographical literature that we have been observing in Wordsworth and Carlyle by comparing them with parallel developments in historiography in the nineteenth century. Since an autobiographical narrative practice seeks to order, and reveal the truth about, "real" past events, it is of a kind with historical narrative *per se*, for the methodological decisions that an autobiographer makes are historiographic as well as literary, novelistic, and poetic ones. It should not be surprising, then, that traditional practices in historiography in the nineteenth century were confronted with a condition of irony that both duplicated and informed the one we have been charting in self-reflexive works.

During the nineteenth century, historiography's growing awareness of the literary and subjective nature of its enterprise led to a kind of epistemological and methodological crisis similar to one we have been charting in the field of autobiography. This "crisis," as Hayden White has shown, had for its "true content" a "condition of irony."[31] The historiographer's growing realization that the content of the history he produced was as much aesthetic and fictional as it was factual and objective, led, as White shows, to the attempt by historical philosophers like Burkhardt, Nietzsche, and Croce, to "dissolve" (41) the irony that seemed inherent in the very practice of writing history. This attempted dissolution spawned a variety of strategic approaches to the philosophy of history during the last third of the nineteenth century.[32] Of all the responses to this condition of irony, none is more relevant to our discussion than Nietzsche's, for Nietzsche did not seek somehow to "explain away" the aesthetic origin of what we take to be historical "fact." Instead, he sought to both affirm and privilege that aesthetic origin by insisting that it was the historian's *task* to be artistic and creative, rather than "scientific," or "objective."

Nietzsche held (in *The Use and Abuse of History*) that since "we require the same artistic vision and absorption in his object

31. Hayden White, *Metahistory: The Historical Imagination in Nineteenth-Century Europe* (Baltimore: Johns Hopkins University Press, 1973), 41. All further references to this work appear in parentheses in the text.

32. See White, *Metahistory*, "Introduction" and "Part One" (1–131). White uses the theory of tropes to analyze the dominant methods of historiography in the nineteenth century, creating what amounts, finally, to a poetics of history or historiography. The three modes, which together amount to a "repudiation" of "Realism" (see Chap. 2), are the metonymical, the metaphorical, and the ironic (represented by Marx, Nietzsche, and Croce respectively).

from the historian" as we do from the artist, "objectivity" for
the historian is a kind of "superstition" or "myth."[33] He insists
that since it is never possible to render a "true picture" of the
past, the historian must strive to create an *artistically* true one:
"To think objectively, in this sense, of history is the work of
the dramatist: to . . . weave the elements [of the past] into a
single whole, with the presumption that the unity of plan must
be put into the objects if it is not already there. So man veils
and subdues the past" (37–38).

Here Carlyle's vision of the artist-as-tailor surfaces in Nietzsche's metaphor of the historian as a kind of artist-weaver. The
"unity of plan" for the aesthetic work of each comes less from
his material than from his own imagination. Thus, for Nietzsche,
the historian requires "above all a great artistic faculty, a creative
vision" (39). The historian "uses" the past, of course, but also
"abuses" it because "the fine historian must have the power of
coining the known into a thing never heard before" (40). In
this process "objectivity" is not dismissed by Nietzsche, but it
is rethought, in White's words, as the goal of "a life-serving
form of art" (352). "Historical wisdom," then, becomes the function not of a traditional conception of objectivity but of an objectivity having its roots in "dramatistic insight" (White, 352).

Nietzsche's philosophical and methodological break with
traditional ideas about history and historiography both mirror
and extend the kinds of changes in self-reflexive works we observed in the thought and practice of Carlyle. The crises of
historicism and of autobiography are both generated by the
same condition of irony, and as such are part of a shifting nineteenth-century epistemology. Thus, as Michel Foucault has
observed in his discussion of Nietzsche's philosophy of history,
Nietzsche's reformulation of the status and practice of histor-

33. Friedrich Nietzsche, *The Use and Abuse of History*, trans. Adrian Col-
lins (Indianapolis: Bobbs-Merrill, 1957), 37. All further references to this work
appear in parentheses in the text.

iography amounts very nearly to the "inverse of the Christian world" view, since it represents a "challenge" to "the pursuit of the origin" that formed the foundation for the "quest" motif in much of western literature.[34] While both the Augustinian and Wordsworthian quests constitute journeys of return that seek to recapture Original knowledge and an Original unity, Foucault points out that Nietzsche's critique of traditional history challenges an epistemology that understands the search for knowledge to be a Wordsworthian search for "primordial truths" (142) whose "lofty origin(s)" (143) can be rediscovered and recovered. Since Nietzsche insisted that the idea of a privileged origin was merely "a metaphysical extension which arises from the belief that things are most precious and essential at the moment of birth,"[35] Foucault concludes that Nietzsche "refuses to extend his faith in metaphysics" to the point of believing that history will "disclose an original identity . . . behind things" (142). Rather, if Nietzsche's new historian "listens to history, he finds that there is 'something altogether different' behind things: not a timeless and essential secret, but the secret that they have no essence or that their essence was fabricated" (142).

What is particularly important for our analysis is Nietzsche's linking, on the one hand, of a belief in the primordial and lofty origins of truth with the traditional historian's production of an objective, factual narrative, and his linking, on the other hand, of a critique of origins with the production of artistic and dramatic—of creative—narratives. This suggests a functional relationship between changing epistemologies and changing

34. Michel Foucault, "Nietzsche, Genealogy, History," reprinted in Michel Foucault, *Language, Counter-Memory, Practice: Selected Essays and Interviews*, trans., ed., Donald F. Bouchard and Sherry Simon (Ithaca: Cornell University Press, 1977), 155, 142, 143. All further references to this work appear in parentheses in the text.

35. Quoted by Foucault in "Nietzsche, Genealogy, History," 143. It is taken from sec. 3 of *The Wanderer and His Shadow* in *The Complete Works of Friedrich Nietzsche*, vol. 7, ed. Oscar Levy (New York: Russell and Russell, 1964).

narrative strategies. What we have seen first in Wordsworth's transposition of Augustine's quest motif into a narrative about natural man's search for his own origins and the source of his original artistic power, and then again in Carlyle's ironic undercutting of the conventions and possibilities of the Wordsworthian retrospective project, is the way in which traditional autobiographical forms began to dissolve as the conventional ideas that underlay their conceptions of subjectivity and its literary representation were dissolving.

The differences between *The Prelude* and *Sartor Resartus* enumerated at the outset of this chapter also surface in Nietzsche's distinction between "historical" and "super-historical" postures toward the past. Foucault's discussion of Nietzsche's distinction (he calls the two categories "traditional" and "effective" approaches to history) emphasizes the epistemological differences underlying the difffering literary approaches of Wordsworth and Carlyle. "Traditional history," Foucault writes, tends to dissolve a "singular event into an ideal continuity," either as part of a "teleological movement or a natural process" (154). Whether it is grounded in a theological (or "teleological") system like Augustine's or a "natural" one like Wordsworth's, "traditional" history treats of the past to "rediscover" it; its "search," therefore, "is directed toward 'that which already was there,' the image of primordial truth," and thus in its quest for "original identity" it "must invoke the objectivity, the accuracy of facts, and the permanence of the past" (158). On the other hand, "effective history" will "never confuse itself with a quest" for the origins of "knowledge," "values," and "morality" in its treatment of the past (144). Rather, "it will uproot its traditional foundations and relentlessly disrupt its pretended continuities" (154). Moreover, "where the soul," Foucault continues, "pretends reunification or the self fabricates a coherent identity" in a search for pure origins, the "effective historian" sets out to "study the beginning" (145) in a way which "does not depend upon 'rediscovery,'" and hence "emphatically excludes the 'rediscovery of ourselves'" (154). Carlyle's *Sartor*, in its guise as personal history, confuses, uproots, and disrupts continuities in just this way, and its irony excludes both the kind of coherent identity, and the quest for its textual realization, represented by the Augustinian and Wordsworthian journeys. Thus, the epistemological changes registered by Carlyle respond both to changing ideas about the subject and to changing ideas about writing historically, or retrospectively.

The implication in *Sartor* that the autobiographical text is always already a fictional history, that artists shape their condition as they write about it, is, in Carlyle's words, a "prophetico-satiric" (185) prefiguration of Nietzsche's notion that the historical text *should*, like its subject, be a consciously aesthetic, imaginative creation. Both writers work their way toward the positing of a creative, or fictional, method for the treatment of past "facts" in discourse, and both do so out of a realization that conventional methods are caught in an irony that undoes their authority. Each shifts creative authority from divinity to the artist, whose fictions are assigned a higher kind of truth than the truth of mere "objectivity."

The result of such a shift, of course, is to open up the autobiographical act to poetic and fictional practices without admitting the self-conscious disturbances which appear in a work like *The Prelude* or the dizzying irony which calls everything in *Sartor* into question. We could turn next, then, to a work like Whitman's *Song of Myself*, where the conceptions of self, poetry, and autobiography are so large, free, and encompassing as to allow its author to use the full sweep of his imagination to create an autobiographical work whose song tries to drown out every hesitation and doubt encountered by Wordsworth or Carlyle. The more useful work to turn to, however, is Joyce's *A Portrait of the Artist as a Young Man*. For Joyce's autobiographical novel represents precisely the kind of historical "dramatization" Nietzsche had in mind. It stands as a complete and conscious reversal of the Augustinian journey, resolves the tension between fact and the imagination in Wordsworth's autobiographical practice into a calmly fictional practice, and it brings to full flower the *Bildungsroman* tradition with which *Sartor* has so many intimate ties. A careful reading of *Portrait* in light of Nietzsche's *Use and Abuse of History* and in contrast to *The Prelude* will reveal both where Joyce's book stands in the history of autobiographical literature and the extent to which it represents a folding of autobiography's practices and purposes into the practices and purposes of the novelist's.

CHAPTER FOUR

A *Portrait of the Artist as a Young Man:* The Art of Fictional Self-Representation

As we, or mother Dana, weave and unweave our bodies, Stephen said, from day to day, their molecules shuttled to and fro, so does the artist weave and unweave his image . . . In the intense instant of imagination . . . that which I was is that which I am and that which in possibility I may come to be. So in the future, the sister of the past, I may see myself as I sit here now but by reflection from that which then I shall be.

—Ulysses

Joyce's weaving and unweaving of his own image in both *Stephen Hero* and *A Portrait of the Artist as a Young Man* recalls Wordsworth's effort in *The Prelude* to compose a retrospective portrait of himself that would make him capable of "building up a work that should endure." However, while these works do share a similar enabling function, Joyce's weaving metaphor suggests that his autobiographical work is methodologically closer to that of the poet-tailor in *Sartor Resartus.* For while Wordsworth resists the conflation of his biographical subject with an imagined one, in Joyce's novel the fictional status of the subject in literary self-representation is a given, and it becomes a point of departure for constructing a narrative that actually depends upon—and exploits—that fictionality. Joyce is not interested, as was Wordsworth, in "faithfully picturing" his past in order to recapture a power thought to reside there. On the contrary, he is interested in imaginatively recasting the past in order to move beyond it.

Embracing such a method, Joyce radically extends what we saw for Wordsworth was only an implicit, and continually repressed, realization that the textual "I" is always partly a fictive Other. In *The Prelude* the irony implicit in literary self-representation asserts itself as an epistemological problem in moments of doubt, and these moments, as we saw, disturb the surface of Wordsworth's poem. In Joyce's novel, on the other hand, the irony of textual self-representation is never discussed as an epistemological problem, since the "problem" itself is avoided by his narrative strategy—to present its subject as, *a priori*, a masked Other. In *The Prelude*, the distance between author and subject raises questions which form part of the poem's subject matter; such questions are continually posed as problems by Wordsworth, but they are necessarily forgotten as the narrative of the "I" moves on relatively unaffected. But in *Portrait*, the distance between author and subject is exploited as a resource. The irony inherent in self-representation is never treated as a "problem" in Joyce's book; it becomes, rather, a central element informing its method.

As we have already seen, the differences underlying these two self-reflexive strategies have their roots both in a changing epistemology of the subject and in changing ideas about the relative factual or fictional status of historical discourse *per se*. In fact the differing methodologies of Wordsworth and Joyce in this regard reflect the differences between "traditional" and "effective" historiographic practices articulated by Nietzsche (and elaborated by Foucault). That is, when compared to Wordsworth's, Joyce's narrative of his own personal history reflects the same break with an earlier nineteenth-century preoccupation with historical "facts" and "origins" as does Nietzsche's break with the traditional practices of historicism. In Joyce's inversion of a Christian world view, epistemology and narrative strategy converge and begin to inform one another. Thus Joyce's book explicitly inverts the Christian quest for a knowledge of origins by fictionalizing those origins, while the story it recounts chronicles its protagonist's attempt to reverse within himself the Christian world view he has inherited.

Thus, in contrast to *The Prelude* (and of course, the *Confessions*), the past in *Portrait* is presented as a series of events grounded in neither a teleological or a natural system but in the will of its protagonist. In the novel, Stephen's will is not directed toward recovery of the past or toward reunification with an original identity but toward uprooting its traditional foundations. Seeking to depict its author's own relationship to his past in this way, *Portrait* inverts the purposes of "traditional" history that, Foucault writes, "seeks the continuities of soil, language, and urban life" (162). In doing so, it becomes a dramatic, "effective" history in the spirit of Nietzsche, a history whose "purpose," in Foucault's summary "is not to discover the roots of our identity, but to commit itself to its dissipation" (162). Intermixing fact and fiction in a dramatization of his own past, Joyce seeks less to chronicle that past than to overcome it.

Although both Wordsworth's poem and Joyce's novel, each in its own way, posit a dialectical relationship between self-knowledge, writing, and self-transformation, the sources of that knowledge are for each writer radically different. Wordsworth, as we have already seen, sought to recount his *return* to, and reconciliation with, an "original" knowledge, an "original" identity and power. Oriented as it is toward what the poet hoped would be a recoverable past and a recuperable lost identity, *The Prelude* seeks to represent the past "as it was," in a narrative voice that insists on—while seeking to achieve—an absolute kind of continuity between the poet's past and present selves. In *Portrait*, on the other hand, Joyce seeks to chronicle his flight from his own identity and his own past. Oriented as it is toward the future and toward the forging of a new artistic "self" born out of a sundering of that self from its past, Joyce's book gives itself over to a willful fictionalization of both the author's past and his own identity, in a way that seeks to create a discontinuity between the author and the past "self" who is the subject of his book.

The picture that emerges, then, when we chart the development of literary self-representation through the texts of Wordsworth, Carlyle, and Joyce, is one of successive adjustments to an emerging realization that autobiographical (and historical) practice is fraught with serious paradoxes. Understood in its relation to a shifting epistemological ground, this realization registers itself not only in the substance of each of these works but in the choices which go toward structuring them. This shift begins to assert itself in *The Prelude* in moments of doubt, which Wordsworth seeks to control by containing them within a purposeful, chronological, ostensibly factual narrative. The shift is raised to the level of crisis by the form of Carlyle's *Sartor*, where the ironic nature of literary self-representation is realized in a text structured to seem manifestly out of control. In *Portrait*, finally, a measure of control is reasserted as Joyce uses a fictional form to avoid the paradoxes that surface in *The Prelude* and *Sartor*, resolving the ontological problems of an autobiographical practice based upon "fact" into an artistic narrative that seeks, *by* its art, to transform a past which it cannot—and does not want to—represent factually.

We can better understand the nature of this effort by examining both the genesis of Joyce's book and the history of its composition. We will find that as his autobiographical method evolved Joyce's interest in presenting an increasingly fictional version of his past grew to parallel his thematic preoccupation with Stephen's need to become an artist by breaking with his past. Joyce began in *Stephen Hero* to render a literal, detailed portrait of his past, but moved on in *Portrait* to transform that past in a more consciously aesthetic and imaginative work of art. When Joyce began early in 1904 to compose an autobiographical portrait of himself, he set about, as the editor of the *Stephen Hero* manuscripts writes, to create "objectively" a "convincing transcript of [his] life."[1] He attempted, that is, to write a somewhat literal, factual, and in its details, historically accurate "autobiography." Thus, as other critics have noted, *Stephen Hero* is "more conventional, discursive, explicit, and unsubtle" than *Portrait*. It is a work, in short, "not yet subject to the restraints and modification of patterned art."[2] Envisioned as a massive work (sixty-three chapters reaching some three hundred thousand words), *Stephen Hero* is filled with incidents and people unmentioned in the later work.[3] With an attention to realistic detail later abandoned in the more streamlined *Portrait*, the earlier book moves from chapter to chapter in what one critic has called "a monotonous chronological succession of events."[4] Written without the clear sense that in writing about himself as a young artist he was giving birth to himself as a mature one, *Stephen Hero* represents Joyce's passive, literal, and strictly retrospective view of his past.

Begun early in 1904, *Stephen Hero* had grown by midsummer into a "large volume."[5] When Joyce and Nora left Dublin for exile in October of that year—making the detachment which he had been chronicling in his book a literal one—he carried with

1. Theodore Spencer, ed., *Stephen Hero*, by James Joyce (Norfolk, Conn.: New Directions, 1963), 10–11.

2. Marvin Magalaner and Richard M. Kain, *Joyce: The Man, the Work, the Reputation* (New York: New York University Press, 1956), 107–8.

3. For more on this kind of comparison between *Stephen Hero* and *Portrait*, see Spencer's "Introduction" to *Stephen Hero*.

4. Hélène Cixous, *The Exile of James Joyce*, trans. Sally A. J. Purcell (New York: David Lewis, 1972), 227.

5. Richard Ellmann, *James Joyce* (New York: Oxford University Press, 1959), 153. Ellmann quotes Joyce's friend C. P. Curran as saying, "The earliest chapters, now lost, were lyrical . . . the tone becoming more bitter and realistic as Joyce proceeded" (153).

him the manuscript of his book, which he continued working on in Zurich, Trieste, and Rome, until by 1907 he had composed some twenty-six chapters.[6] But in the middle of 1907 Joyce's conception of his book changed. He began to rework it into the much sparser, more highly fictionalized *Portrait*.

This change had much to do with his growing realization that by writing about his growth as an artist he might become one. This realization coincided with the birth of his daughter Lucia Anne in July 1907. Joyce was in the hospital for treatment of rheumatism when Nora was admitted, and they spent their convalescences together with Joyce meditating "on the parallel between artistic conception and gestation and their human equivalent."[7] Joyce, as Richard Ellmann records, had been very much interested in the process of gestation since Nora's first pregnancy, and it was apparently during summer 1907 that this early interest, coupled with a vague sense that human character developed like an "embryo," coalesced into a theory of artistic creation.[8]

The development of this theory contributed to Joyce's decision to begin his autobiographical narrative anew. His turn from a more literal transcription of his past to a fictional recreation of it in *Portrait* represents Joyce's new understanding that the artist's imagination, not his memory, is what must guide his work. Animated by the new sense that in writing about himself he was not remembering himself as a "hero" but creating himself as an "artist," Joyce set out in *Portrait* to become "the

6. The manuscripts of *Stephen Hero* suffered as much as the author who wrote them. Some were thrown in a fire by Joyce, fortunately to be rescued by his wife. Others, Joyce claimed, were sold to someone in the United States. See Spencer's "Introduction" to *Stephen Hero*.

7. Cixous, *Exile*, 422.

8. Ellmann notes that, according to Joyce's brother Stanislaus, Joyce "thought of a man's character as developing 'from an embryo' with constant traits." "Joyce acted upon this theory," Ellmann continues, "with his characteristic thoroughness, and his subsequent interest in the process of gestation, as conveyed to Stanislaus during Nora's first pregnancy, expressed a concern that was literary as well as anatomical" (*Joyce*, 307).

artist forging anew in his workshop out of the sluggish matter of the earth a new soaring impalpable imperishable being."[9] In re-conceiving his autobiographical effort (in figures of gestation and birth) Joyce found both a metaphor for the story in *Portrait* and a structuring principle for his autobiographical novel. Thus, Ellmann has observed,

> *A Portrait of the Artist as a Young Man* is in fact the gestation of a soul, and in the metaphor Joyce found his new principle of order. The book begins with Stephen's father and, just before the ending, it depicts the hero's severance from his mother . . . in the first chapter the foetal soul is for a few pages only slightly individualized . . . the being struggles toward some unspecified, uncomprehended culmination . . . In the third chapter . . . conscience develops . . . Then at the end of the fourth chapter the soul discovers the goal towards which it has been mysteriously proceeding . . . The final chapter shows the soul, already fully developed, fattening itself for its journey . . . In the last few pages of the book . . . the soul is released from its confinement, its individuality is complete, and the style shifts with savage abruptness.[10]

Ellmann was the first to understand the paradoxical implications of such a marriage of theory and practice: in fashioning a narrative in which he gives "birth" to himself, Joyce in effect becomes "his own mother."[11]

With this new kind of approach guiding his autobiographical project, Joyce began to rework *Stephen Hero*, reducing its twenty-six chapters into what became five parts in *Portrait*. In doing so he began to take a more revisionary approach toward the writing of "autobiography": his own past now existed not as a fixed set of experiences to be recaptured but as material to be reworked in what he called in *Portrait* the "womb" of his

9. James Joyce, *A Portrait of the Artist as a Young Man* (New York: Viking, 1964), 169. All further references appear in parentheses in the text.
10. Ellmann, *Joyce*, 307.
11. Ibid., 309.

imagination (217). In his transition from *Stephen Hero* to *Portrait*, Joyce's writing about his past turns, like Wordsworth's, into an attempt to perpetuate the story that it recounts. While *Portrait* chronicles Stephen's growing sense of the "distance" between himself and his own personal and cultural pasts (a distance he eventually comes to nurture), the growing aesthetic distance between Joyce and Stephen in the successive versions of his book becomes an extension, a continuation, of Joyce's ongoing struggle to detach himself both from his past and from his past self.[12] If this detachment is analogous, as Ellmann suggests, to the process of giving birth to a "new" artistic self, then the detachment from his past represented by Joyce's conscious decision in 1907 to wholly make it over by fictionalizing it also constitutes his attempt to create an aesthetic distance that parallels the actual distance he put between himself and his past when he went into exile three years earlier.

We should remember that the relationship between exile and Stephen's efforts to become an artist by moving beyond the "nets" of his own past is the one which draws the book to a close. Near the end of *Portrait*, Stephen links his liberation from his past to his ability as an artist to express himself, declaring that in this struggle he will use for his "defence" the "only arms" he knows—"silence, exile, and cunning" (247). "Exile" represents in *Portrait* the final detachment toward which the whole of Stephen's experience has been tending. Envisioned as a kind of necessary liberation, however, Joyce's actual exile from Dublin became less a break with his past than the achieving of a comfortable, creative distance from it. The aesthetic distance that Joyce introduced into his autobiographical narrative after his exile, then, extends the need for distance represented by that exile into the very method of his book: just

12. The question of "esthetic distance" in *Portrait* is treated at some length by Chester G. Anderson, Wayne Booth, and Robert Scholes in the Viking Critical Library edition *A Portrait of the Artist as a Young Man: Text, Criticism, and Notes*, ed. Chester G. Anderson (New York: Penguin, 1977), 446–80.

as he needed the actual distance between Dublin and Trieste in order to return to his past to rewrite it, Joyce came to need the aesthetic distance he finally created in his autobiographical narrative between his protagonist and himself in order to "recreate" himself as an artist. Both kinds of distance came to form a single context integral to Joyce's fictional treatment of his own past, a treatment he conceived as a necessary prelude to his career as a writer.

The convergence of Joyce's work and life in what was meant to be an authorizing self-reflexive narrative constituted, as Ellmann writes, "the extraordinary beginning of Joyce's mature work" (149). Though Joyce's "beginning" was launched with more brashness and egoism than Wordsworth's, his consciousness of the relationship between the purposeful composition of an autobiographical "portrait" and the beginning of his mature career parallels the poet's.[13] Both narratives, it should be noted, are nearly archetypal examples of what Said has called "beginning texts," narratives that are about, and that at the same time seek to enact, the individual's search for a new beginning for the self, born out of a consciousness of the need for "reversal,

13. Wordsworth was well aware that *The Prelude* was an egotistical project. He wrote to George Beaumont near its completion that it is "a thing unprecedented in literary history that a man should talk so much about himself" (Ernest de Selincourt, ed., *The Early Letters of William and Dorothy Wordsworth (1787–1805)* [Oxford: Clarendon, 1935], 489). However, he went on to insist that "it is not self-conceit, as you will know well, that has induced me to do this, but real humility." As this last remark suggests, Wordsworth sought quite consciously to avoid the appearance of egotism. In his letters he often scolds himself for lapsing into what seem innocent enough descriptions of his "outrageous egotism" (*Early Letters*, 61); in another he apologizes for having "again relapsed into egotism" (*Early Letters*, 36), and in yet another he writes, "I am extremely rude . . . to talk so much about myself" (*Early Letters*, 48). Joyce, on the other hand, was known for his brashness and his egotism, which he used quite consciously to make his way in the world. In *Stephen Hero*, he writes that he had an "ingenuous" and willfully contrived "arrogance" (125) and a "taste for enigmatic roles" (77). Elsewhere in the novel he speaks of his "ineradicable egoism," an egoism that, he writes, "he was afterwards to call redeemer" (34).

change of direction," and "discontinuity."[14] These "reversals," for Said, are pursued in the activity of writing a "beginning text," so that the plot of the *self's* new beginning is reflected in the artist's *textual* one. These narratives, written "for the purpose of forging the beginning" of their authors' careers (45), tend to provide that beginning by chronicling it. Thus, while narratives like *The Prelude* and *Portrait* seek to recount their authors' "conversion" (or in Wordsworth's sense, reconversion) to a literary career, it is the act of composing those narratives that most crucially helps them to (re)enact it.

"Beginning," in Said's sense of the word, is a concept that comprehends both the crisis overcome in the story of these narratives, and the new beginning announced by their composition. In the activity of composition, "The writer's life, his career, and his text form a system of relationships whose configuration *in real human time* becomes progressively stronger. . . . In fact, these relationships gradually become the writer's all-encompassing subject. On a pragmatic level, then, his text is his statement of the temporal course of his career, inscribed in language, and shot through and through with precisely these matters" (227).[15] Both *The Prelude* and *Portrait*, "shot through and through with precisely these matters" become absolute examples of how "beginning texts" can become in the end what Said calls "pure sign(s) of the writer's career" (223).

Fictional in form though it may be, Joyce's book is not without the need to be "objective" about its author's past. Its objectivity, however, is the objectivity of Nietzsche's dramatic historian, who seeks to give the past a measure of truth by rendering it in an aesthetic form. Although it seems paradoxical, Joyce in-

14. Edward W. Said, *Beginnings: Intention and Method* (Baltimore: Johns Hopkins University Press, 1975), 34. All further references to this work appear in parentheses in the text.

15. It should be pointed out that "on a pragmatic level" this passage also describes Augustine's *Confessions*. A deconstructive reading of Augustine's narrative, one that sought to analyze the rhetorical strategy underlying its metaphysical language, would reveal it as *the* "beginning text" *par excellence*.

tended *Portrait* to be both fictive *and* factual—to be, as he put
it to Frank Budgen, "candid": "Many writers have written about
themselves. I wonder if any of them has been as candid as I
have?"[16] In moving from the more traditionally objective *Stephen
Hero* to the more fictional *Portrait*, Joyce moved toward the
writing of a self-history with dramatistic insight. In *Portrait*,
S. L. Goldberg writes, Joyce "created an autobiographical drama.
. . . Stephen's consciousness was both the stage and the protagonist of the drama, and its growth was the action."[17] Joyce's
new rationale for the "autobiographical art" of *Portrait*, Goldberg writes, is to avoid *Stephen Hero*'s monotonous depiction of
"the merely chronological sequence of the artist's activities,"
and to focus, rather, on Stephen's "inner drama," on the "implicit form and significance" of his experience.[18]

In this refashioning of his narrative, Joyce actually returned
to the original conception of literary portraiture outlined in his
1904 "Portrait" essay, from which both versions of his autobiographical work grew:

> The features of infancy are not commonly reproduced in the
> adolescent portrait for, so capricious are we, that we cannot
> or will not conceive the past in any other than its iron memorial
> aspect. Yet the past assuredly implies a fluid succession of pres-
> ents, the development of an entity of which our actual present
> is a phase only. Our world, again, recognises its acquaintance
> chiefly by the characters of beard and inches and is, for the most
> part, estranged from those of its members who seek through
> some art, by some process of the mind as yet untabulated, to
> liberate from the personalized lumps of matter that which is
> their individuating rhythm, the first or formal relation of their
> parts. But for such as these a portrait is not an identificative
> paper but rather the curve of an emotion.[19]

16. Quoted in Maurice Beebe, "The Artist as Hero," in *A Portrait of the
Artist as a Young Man: Text, Criticism, and Notes*, ed. Anderson, 71.

17. S. L. Goldberg, *James Joyce* (New York: Grove, 1962), 48.

18. Ibid., 18–19.

19. Reprinted in Robert E. Scholes and Richard M. Kain, eds., *The Workshop of Daedalus: James Joyce and the Raw Materials for A Portrait of the
Artist as a Young Man* (Evanston: Northwestern University Press, 1965), 60.

Here we have a sense of both the thematic texture and the structural design we encounter in *Portrait*, where such matters as estrangement, individuation, liberation, art, and formal aesthetic relations will be woven together in a way that seeks less to be an "identificative paper" than to register the prolonged "curve of emotion." As a narrative that seeks to extend the artist's efforts at self-liberation into the very time and activity of writing, *Portrait* returns to this early notion that a self-portrait should "liberate," rather than simply "identify," its subject. This extension affirms by example Joyce's observation that the "actual present is a phase only" of the past, since writing to liberate the self is the present phase in a "fluid succession" of *past* efforts to liberate himself.

Joyce's assertion in the "Portrait" essay that it is "through some art," some "process of the mind," that the artist's individuality is "liberated," is of course an extension of the same idea that we have already encountered in Hegel and Carlyle. Joyce's conception here, however, is much closer to Carlyle's than to Hegel's. For Carlyle's conception of what Hegel calls the artist's "practical activity" is, as we have already seen, rooted in the "actual," in the writer's very worldly labors. Moreover, it disassociates itself from the overtly religious conception of Hegel, who views the essential nature of the mind, and its processes, as divine. Joyce's conception of the artist's creative process also becomes disassociated from Hegel's, but by way of a half-serious, half-ironic, appropriation of Hegel's language of transcendence. While Hegel insists that in creating a work of art the mind performs a "baptism of the spiritual" on what it has "moulded," Joyce describes his art in *Portrait* as the "transmuting of the daily bread of experience into the radiant body of everliving life" (221). Joyce is clearly speaking metaphorically— and surely, partly with tongue in cheek, for his use of the language of the church is an act not of doctrinal allegiance but of appropriation. As Ellmann has observed, Joyce left the Catholic church not so much by denying it as by "transmuting" its language for his own uses: "Christianity had subtly evolved in his mind from a religion into a system of metaphors, which as metaphors could claim his fierce allegiance. . . . He converted the temple to new uses instead of trying to knock it down."[20]

Joyce's new method in *Portrait*, then, turned the monotonous reportage of *Stephen Hero* into the purposeful aesthetic enterprise of transmuting "personalised lumps" of past experience into a literary portrait that would register the "curve" of its protagonist's "emotions." It is this attempted transmutation that more than anything else is finally responsible for the structural design of *Portrait*, for in both the quality and the curve of the transitions between the book's five parts can be seen Joyce's attempted dramatization of the emotional rhythm of Stephen's individuation. It is this method that replaces *Stephen Hero's* "monotonous chronological succession of events" in which "one incident seems as important as the next."[21] In *Portrait*, the monotony of *Stephen Hero's* chronology is replaced by a rhythm of oscillation, as Stephen moves between each end of an emotional curve; from an emotional "high" back down to the actual and harsh realities of circumstance. Stephen's repeated movement between triumph and trial represents Joyce's creation of a structural design meant to reproduce the sometimes turbulent rhythm of the process of Stephen's individuation, and the troubled growth of his mind.

Since Joyce sought to revise the detailed biographical experiences in *Stephen Hero* into an artistic pattern that might dramatize the rhythm of his own individuation, he had to focus on the most central aspects of his growth as an "artist." Appropriately enough, he redesigned his book to foreground, in a subtle yet patterned way, the development of his relationship to language. Joyce thus was able to balance the dramatization of the "inner world" of Stephen's "emotions" with a dramatiza-

20. Ellmann, *Joyce*, 68.
21. Magalaner and Kain, *Joyce: The Man, the Work, the Reputation*, 108.

tion of the "inner world" of his developing intellect. In Joyce's redesigned autobiographical narrative, Stephen becomes a journeying soul, and the topography over which he travels becomes the confusing, and yet the finally liberating, terrain of language itself. It is *this* story that defines Joyce's past as an extended prelude to his becoming a writer.

By choosing to foreground the growth of Stephen's relationship to language in *Portrait*, Joyce affirmed in practice his assertion that "the first step in the direction of truth is . . . to comprehend the act itself of intellection" (208). The desire to achieve this kind of comprehension animates Stephen's journey in *Portrait*, where the "act itself of intellection" is dramatized in Stephen's struggle to understand and then control the relationship between language and knowing. From the very beginning of *Portrait*, language is the "womb" in which the "gestation" of Stephen's soul takes place.[22] In its opening pages, Joyce links the development of Stephen's consciousness to his growing comprehension that words exist in and of themselves as sensuous objects; he realizes that by associating and linking them together, we in effect create our own world. The development of his comphrension quickly becomes a part of the book's plot line: Stephen's journey through the world of language parallels, indeed it forms an integral part of, the journey of his soul away from the past and toward a new "reality of experience" forged in "the smithy" of his soul (253). Consistent with the change in style from *Stephen Hero*, Joyce does not so much talk about the nature of this journey as he attempts to dramatize it in the method of his narration. Stephen's very early recognition, for instance, that the word "belt" has multiple meanings dawns on the reader in nearly the same way as it dawned on Stephen:

> He crept about from point to point on the fringe of his line, making little runs now and then. But his hands were bluish with

22. On the important role of language in Stephen's developing consciousness in *Portrait*, see Cixious, *Exile*, 359–433 passim, and Dorothy Van Ghent, *The English Novel: Form and Function* (New York: Holt, Rinehart and Winston, 1953), 263–76.

cold. He kept his hands in the sidepockets of his belted grey
suit. That was a belt round his pocket. And belt was also to
give a fellow a belt. One day a fellow had said to Cantwell:—
I'd give you such a belt in a second. Cantwell answered:—Go
and fight your match. Give Cecil Thunder a belt. [9]

This scene follows the movement of his consciousness from the
tactile to the remembered in a way that seeks to dramatize
Stephen's actual experience of this association. As he does regularly in *Portrait*, Joyce here effects a subtle transition in the
focus of his narration—from the consciousness of the narrator to
Stephen's. This transition does not happen *in fact* of course—
the narration strictly speaking always remains in the third person—but it happens in *effect*, an effect signaled by a qualitative
change in the speaker's language to reflect the language of a
young boy. Thus, the transition from "He kept his hands in the
sidepockets of his belted grey suit," to "That was a belt round
his pocket. And belt was also to give a fellow a belt," dramatizes
the beginning of Stephen's association by a change in the focus
of the narration, one that brings the reader "in" to Stephen's
consciousness at the very moment he is making the association.

In dramatizing these associative experiences Joyce attempts
to capture Stephen's sense of confusion about them as well as
his perplexity over the feelings they elicit from him:

Suck was a queer word . . . [and] the sound was ugly. Once he
had washed his hands in the lavatory . . . and his father pulled
the stopper . . . and the dirty water went down through the
hole . . . [and] had made a sound like that: suck. Only louder.
To remember that and the white look of the lavatory made
him feel cold and then hot. There were two cocks that you
turned and water came out: cold and hot. He felt cold and then
a little hot: and he could see the names printed on the cocks.
That was a very queer thing. [11]

This is one of many examples in the book of the way in which
words—as "suck" does here—begin to materialize for Stephen
as actual, sensuous things. The process of this sensualization is

depicted in Stephen's association of this "queer" word with the sound of water going down the drain. The memory of this experience explains why "suck" seems a "queer" word to Stephen, and it also triggers a further remembering of an even stranger association, that of relating his feeling "cold and then hot" to the names on the water faucets. *That* was a queer thing because the association between words and feelings was both uncanny and inexplicable: evident, but out of his conscious control, and thus beyond his understanding.

Stephen's growing awareness, however, of the relationship between these kinds of associations and the act of *knowing* develops into a further understanding that his own intellect can form these associations for itself. This is what Stephen comes to comprehend when he thinks puzzlingly about the phrase "Tower of Ivory" from the Catholic litany:

> [Dante] did not like him to play with Eileen because Eileen was a protestant and when she was young she knew children that used to play with protestants and the protestants used to make fun of the litany of the Blessed Virgin. *Tower of Ivory*, they used to say, *House of Gold!* How could a woman be a tower of ivory or a house of gold? [35]

An image from Stephen's memory rushes into his mind at this point as he makes the following association:

> Eileen had long white hands. One evening when playing tig she had put her hands over his eyes: long and white and thin and cold and soft. That was ivory: a cold white thing. That was the meaning of *Tower of Ivory*. [36]

The association here between "Ivory" and "woman" is not so "queer" a thing precisely because Stephen is making it for himself. The "meaning" of the phrase is made by him in a more or less voluntary effort of his intellect. The measure he exerts here over the relationship between signifier ("Ivory") and signified ("woman") leads him a little later, as he repeats it, to a central, if elementary, realization:

. . . [A]ll of a sudden [Eileen] had broken away and had run laughing down the sloping curve of the path. Her fair hair had streamed out behind her like the gold in the sun. *Tower of Ivory. House of Gold.* By thinking of things you could understand them. [43].

With this conscious insight, Stephen has moved from a perplexity about the play of words and their "queer" associations to a beginning effort at understanding "the act itself of intellection." As his life in language begins to unfold in a more conscious kind of way, words themselves soon become Stephen's chief link to reality even though he may not know what all of them mean:

Words which he did not understand he said over and over to himself till he had learned them by heart: and through them he had glimpses of the real world about him. [62]

Joyce's recurrent foregrounding of language in Stephen's developing consciousness in the opening pages of *Portrait* works, of course, to form a logical prelude to the recounting of his early aspirations to be a poet. Joyce's book, after all, is a portrait of the writer as a young man, and his depiction of Stephen's early self-consciousness about the relationship between language and knowing is meant to dramatize one of the earliest stages of his artistic development. In moving from Stephen's realization that the associative power of language is a plastic one—that "by thinking of things you could understand them"— to his first attempt at actually writing poetry, we move more deeply into the drama of Stephen's individuation as an artist.

This drama is generated out of the tension Stephen experiences between what we might call on the one hand, after Eliot, tradition, and on the other hand, individual talent. Note the way in which Joyce emphasizes Stephen's dependence on tradition in the composition of his first poem:

Before him lay a new pen, a new bottle of ink and a new emerald exercise [book]. From force of habit he had written at the top

of the first page the initial letters of the jesuit motto: A.M.D.G.
["for the greater glory of God"]. On the first line of the page appeared the title of the verses he was trying to write: to E—C—.
He knew it was right to begin so for he had seen similar titles
in the collected poems of Lord Byron. [70]

Stephen's writing table is arranged here as if for some ritual.
The artist that Stephen will later strive to become is here the
fledgling poet who by "force of habit" seeks for his art the
invocation of the Word and who strives to be formally correct
in the manner of Byron. His attention to mannered details belies
the hollowness of his efforts. Joyce's description of the sparse
and nearly lifeless poem Stephen creates serves to emphasize
how his dependence on traditionally stylized forms (and the
sources of their authority) hampers his ability to translate something of life into his art:

> There remained no trace of the tram itself nor of the trammen
> nor of the horses: nor did he and she appear vividly. The verses
> told only of the night and the balmy breeze and the maiden
> lustre of the moon. Some unidentified sorrow was hidden in
> the hearts of the protagonists as they stood in silence between
> the leafless trees. [70–71]

Stephen's poem is a pale figure of the "epiphany" from Joyce's
notebook on which it is based:

> The children who have stayed latest are getting on their things
> to go home for the party is over. This is the last tram. The lank
> brown horses know it and shake their bells to the clear night,
> in admonition. The conductor talks with the driver; both nod
> often in the green light of the lamp. There is nobody near. We
> seem to listen, I on the upper step and she on the lower. She
> comes up to my step many times and goes down again, between
> our phrases, and once or twice remains beside me, forgetting to
> go down, and then goes down . . . Let be; let be . . . And now
> she does not urge her vanities—her fine dress and sash and long
> black stockings—for now (wisdom of children) we seem to know

that this end will please us better than any end we have laboured for.[23]

The subtle evocation of the emotion of this moment in Joyce's careful description of detail and physical movement is characteristic of his "epiphany" form. Seen in contrast to the poem he has Stephen write, it emphasizes the vapidness of Stephen's overly formal lyric. (It also reminds us that as a maturing artist Joyce evolved his own, more personal "lyric" form beyond the formal structures of the poem.) The inadequacy of Stephen's poem is particularized and made more explicit when he recalls, a few pages later, the occasion of its composition—his goodbye to Emma on the tram. He observes that he composed the verses about this leavetaking because of "the stream of moody emotions it had made to course through him" (77). But this moodiness, he continues, "had not found an outlet in verse," since "the stream of gloomy tenderness within him had started forth and returned upon itself in dark courses and eddies, wearying him in the end" (77). The "failure" of Stephen's poem marks an important point in Joyce's book. By suggesting that poetry might actually become an "outlet" for Stephen's moodiness, Joyce posits a therapeutic kind of relationship between language and the self.

At this point however, as Stephen notes, the "outlet" which is writing is "stopped up"; the stream of his gloom "starts forth," but returns to him in eddies once again. This blockage is in part due to the incongruity between the nature of his own emotions and the stylized and hollow form of the verses he composes to release them. When he is able, later in the book, to achieve a more effective kind of poetic release, it is only after he explicitly has begun to detach himself from the traditional "voices" of authority that have surrounded him:

. . . [H]e had heard about him the constant voices of his father and of his masters, urging him to be a gentleman above all

23. Quoted in Scholes and Kain, *Workshop of Daedalus*, 13.

things and urging him to be a good catholic above all things. These voices had now come to be hollowsounding in his ears. . . . And it was the din of all these hollowsounding voices that made him bolt irresolutely in the pursuit of phantoms. He gave them ear only for a time but he was happy only when he was far from them, beyond their call, alone or in the company of phantasmal comrades. [83–84]

Joyce characteristically focuses here as much upon the *language* of authority as upon authority itself, since Stephen's individuation as a writer depends throughout *Portrait* on his growing recognition of the crucial relationship between the two. In order to forge for himself his own authoritative voice, he must first detach himself from a constraining relationship to figures of authority in his past, a detachment that is preceded by his break with their language and with the rhetoric of their authority. Thus, this initial and tentative awakening to the need to be "far" away from the "hollowsounding voices" of his father and his masters is the first stirring of his later need to "fly by" the "nets" of home and church by seeking exile from them.

This declaration is followed a few pages later by a more effective attempt on Stephen's part to use the rhythm of language as an outlet for his emotions. Filled "with a strange dread" on the night train to Cork, Stephen

prayed that the day might come quickly. His prayer, addressed neither to God nor saint, began with a shiver . . . and ended in a trail of foolish words which he made to fit the insistent rhythm of the train; and silently, at intervals of four seconds, the telegraph poles held the galloping notes of the music between punctual bars. This furious music allayed his dread and, leaning against the window-ledge, he let his eyelids close again. [87]

This curious prayer, with no "hollowsounding" invocation to God, is more like a poem, a poem composed to allay Stephen's restless dread. Its words are not stylized but "foolish," its form not mannered after the work of another poet but embodying the very rhythm of the experience that is evoking it. In the rhythm and the music of his "poem," Stephen has given a freer and unfettered rein to his imagination. Consequently, his language does not "eddy" in "dark courses" that eventually return his dread to him. Rather it "gallops" his dread away in "notes" and "punctual bars." Here the therapeutic relationship between language and the self is reiterated, but this time "poetry" is transformed by Stephen's growing imagination into a momentarily effective outlet for the stream of his emotions.

The context in which the changing nature of Stephen's relationship to language becomes explicit is important. It is on his visit with his father to Cork that Stephen realizes that his "childhood was dead or lost" (96). Death exists in *Portrait* as a recurrent image of the various stages of Stephen's individuation—appropriately, since his movement is traced as a continuous movement away from his past, a "dying" into a new, mysterious present. Thus the sense here that his past is "dead" is bracketed by his earlier sense at Clongowes that he was dying, that he was beginning to "fade out like a film in the sun" ("He . . . had wandered out of existence for he no longer existed" [93]), and his sense a little later as he listens to the famous sermon on hell that "the film of death" was "veiling" his eyes, that "the bright centres" of his "brain [were being] extinguished one by one like lamps" (112).

The realization at Cork that his childhood was either dead or lost marks a crucial stage in Stephen's individuation, since it is the point at which he begins consciously to throw off both his "dead" past *and* its dead language. This throwing off does not, of course, come without a struggle—a struggle mediated once again by language. When "the memory of his childhood suddenly grew dim," Joyce writes, Stephen

   . . . could scarcely recognize as his his own thoughts, and repeated slowly to himself:
   —I am Stephen Dedalus. I am walking beside my father whose name is Simon Dedalus. We are in Cork, in Ireland.

> Cork is a city. Our room is in the Victoria Hotel. Victoria and
> Stephen and Simon. Simon and Stephen and Victoria. Names.
> [92]

Here Stephen tries to "glimpse" reality through its names, to
reorient himself by naming the present. Turning from these
names in the present, Stephen begins to search through his
memory for some glimpse of himself, but as "he tried to call
forth" some "vivid moments" from his past, his consciousness
failed him. He could recall "only names: Dante, Parnell, Clane,
Clongowes" (92–93). Both of these attempts to "recover," to
re-identify himself, become futile. "His mind," Joyce writes,
"seemed older" than his father's and his father's friends (95):
"He was in another world: he had awakened from a slumber of
centuries" (100).

Stephen envisions his withdrawal from his own past and his
embracing of the "reality of experience" as a kind of "destiny,"
one in which he would progressively and consciously become
"elusive of social or religious orders" (162).[24] This growing realization, as we have seen, is accompanied by the conviction that
he must also become "elusive" of the "order" constituted by their
languages. Thus, Joyce writes that during this period Stephen
felt not only "as though he were slowly passing out of an accus-
tomed world," but also that he was "hearing its language for the
last time" (156).

After Stephen's rejection of the priesthood in Part 4, his
conscious break with traditional sources of order—and his concomitant detachment from the sources of that order in lan-

24. Stephen's observation here is reflected quite pointedly by Joyce in a
letter to Nora in August 1904, when he writes that "Six years ago I left the
Catholic Church, hating it most fervently . . . I made secret war upon it when
I was a student and declined to accept the positions it offered me. By doing
this I made mself a beggar but I retained my pride. Now I make open war
upon it by what I write and say and do. I cannot enter the social order except
as a vagabond" (*Selected Letters of James Joyce*, ed. Richard Ellmann [New
York: Viking, 1975], 25–26).

guage—accelerates: "His own consciousness of language," Joyce writes, "was ebbing" away from him (179). Walking through Dublin, Stephen's exile from the language around him seems to prefigure the actual exile he will embrace some seventy-four pages later:

> . . . [H]e found himself glancing from one casual word to another on his right or left in stolid wonder that they had been so silently emptied of instantaneous sense until every mean shop legend bound his mind like the words of a spell and his soul shrivelled up, sighing with age as he walked on in a lane among heaps of dead language. [178–79]

In linking the "shrivelling" of Stephen's soul to the "heaps of dead language" surrounding it, Joyce emphasizes the relationship he is drawing between the self and the language with which it is constituted. The reconstitution of self, and the reconstitution of language, are becoming for Stephen two aspects of a single activity: the growth of the poet's mind. However, Stephen's break with the past and its language is becoming less a break *per se* than a kind of displacement, the displacement of one kind of tradition for another. At this stage in the "gestation" of the artist's soul, language remains for Stephen both the very stuff *of* consciousness and the material from which he is forging his consciousness as an artist. In this displacement, however, it is no longer the "hollowsounding" language of his father or the "dried up sources" of the language of the church fathers that permeates his consciousness; now it is the language of those writers who are becoming his *poetic* fathers (152). Thus, Joyce's earlier observation that it was through "words which he did not understand" that Stephen "had glimpses of the real world about him" comes to have its analogue in Part 5 in Joyce's description of his walk to the University:

> The rain laden trees of the avenue evoked in him, as always, memories of the girls and women in the plays of Gerhart Hauptmann . . . he foreknew that as he passed the sloblands of Fair-

view he would think of the cloistal silverveined prose of Newman
. . . he would recall the dark humour of Guido Cavalcanti . . .
the spirit of Ibsen would blow through him like a keen wind . . .
[and] he would repeat the song by Ben Jonson which begins:

I was not wearier where I lay.

[176]

Stephen's individuation, which is by now a part of his conscious development of an individual artistic perspective, is still
growing in relationship to a past. But it is a past not of his
family, his church, or his nation; it is an individually selected—
and therefore a somewhat eclectic—literary past, drawn from
sources of authority that "blow through him like a keen wind."
Stephen's attempt to become independent of his past has become incorporated in a much wider attempt to create for himself
another "artistic" past he can depend on. At this stage in his
growth as an artist, the life of Stephen's mind and the language
of the artists with whom he feels a kinship have merged into
one. Such a merger vivifies the way in which his growth has
eclipsed the language of his personal and his cultural pasts. In
the final analysis, Stephen's bold declaration of his intention to
go into exile is only the last in a series of efforts to turn away
from the "hollowsounding voices" of a language whose authority
he is trying to reject:

> I will not serve that in which I no longer believe whether it
> *call itself* my home, my fatherland or my church: and I will
> try to express myself in some mode of life or art as freely as I
> can and as wholly as I can, using for my defence the only arms I
> allow myself to use—silence, exile, and cunning. [246–47; my
> emphasis]

Stephen's exile will not be simply from "home," "fatherland,"
or "church"; it will be an exile from a rhetoric of authority signified by these names: the names themselves have finally become
for him like "hollowsounding voices" of authority. To express
himself he must seek a mode of art free from their rhetoric.

The break with his past represented by Joyce's exile is, as we noted earlier, less a break than the creation of a necessary distance between the artist and his "fatherland." The transition that *Portrait* charts in Stephen's consciousness as he methodically exchanges an inherited attachment to his personal and social pasts for an attachment to a literary and mythical one is, in fact, figured in his movement from one father to another. *Portrait* opens with Stephen's actual father telling him a story; it closes with a plea to his "new father" for the power he needs to tell his *own* story: "Old father, old artificer, stand me now and ever in good stead" (253). Joyce himself, of course, is to be that "artificer," exiled from father and fatherland, so that he can transform his past by rewriting it. Hence, while Ellmann is right in his observation that by giving "birth" to his book Joyce has become his own "mother," there is also a sense in which by the same activity he seeks to become his own father. By becoming the "artificer" of his own past, Joyce has usurped what Stephen calls in *Ulysses* the "legal fiction" of "paternity" (207). To the extent to which Joyce, in creating Stephen, is giving birth to himself, he has fashioned a creative process in which he becomes son and father, as well as mother to himself. Like Shakespeare's playing King Hamlet in Stephen's equation in *Ulysses*, Joyce, by "playing" Stephen in *Portrait*, is both "the ghost and the prince"—the father and the son (*Ulysses*, 212). And like Shakespeare's father, Joyce's lies "disarmed of fatherhood" after *Portrait*, having been usurped of this "mystical estate" by his own son (*Ulysses*, 207). The mother's "womb" may be the metaphorical place in which Stephen's "gestation" in *Portrait* occurs, but the struggle of his birth is a struggle over authority and it takes place in the context of a complex tension between past and present, a tension in which the artist stuggles to become not a son of his past, but its father.[25]

25. The whole of the library scene in *Ulysses* constitutes an interesting commentary on Joyce's own autobiographical project, since the central discussion orchestrated by Stephen concerns the "autobiographical" elements of

The preoccupation in *Portrait* with the development of Stephen's consciousness and with his life in language is of course a reflection of its author's preoccupation with dramatizing the central elements of his own development and growth as a writer. The book is a dramatic, an imaginative, a fictional autobiography precisely because it seeks to chronicle its protagonist's developing relationship to language as a tool for the *imagination's* creative and dramatic powers. Conceived in part as Joyce's way of justifying his pretensions as an artist and written in part as an exercise enabling him to begin such a vocation, *Portrait* re-imagines its author's past in order to overcome it. Its strategy is, in the end, opposed to Wordsworth's, since it does not intend to recapture the past for the purposes of a recovery but to overcome the past for the purposes of making a willful new beginning in exile from it. As Goldberg has aptly said, *Portrait* is about "a self partly outgrown, yet also, in the writing of the book, now partly fulfilled."[26]

In the final analysis such a fulfillment represents on Joyce's part a systemization of Carlyle's insights about the inherently fictive status of the self-reflexive subject. For what was in *Sartor Resartus* an assertion about the inherently creative nature of autobiographical writing becomes a full-blown method in *Portrait*. Joyce's book returns to the form of chronological narration utilized by Wordsworth but with the subject depicted less as a faithful picture than as an artistically imagined portrait. While the novel evolves out of an autobiographical impulse akin to Wordsworth's, Joyce composes his own portrait with a post-Carlylean creative license that sharply distinguishes the book's method from that of its Romantic precursor.

Shakespeare's plays. For Stephen, the "autobiographical backdrop" that he posits for some of the plays is crucial to an understanding of the kind of "reconciliation" the later ones are striving for. It is also central to his delineation of the relationship between writing, fathering, and the creative power of God. See *Ulysses* (New York: Random House, 1961), 184–218 passim.

26. Goldberg, *James Joyce*, 49.

CHAPTER FIVE

Self-Representation and the Limits of Narrative

Having taken an extended look at Joyce's *Portrait* and the ways in which its fictional form seeks to avoid the representational problems encountered by Wordsworth and thematized by Carlyle, we now can examine more closely the theoretical assumptions that underlie the choice of such a strategy. We can do this by probing further into Joyce's autobiographical project and the aesthetic ideas that inform it, comparing them to *Portrait*'s most famous counterpart, Proust's *A la recherche du temps perdu*. For together, as Said has observed, "Proust and Joyce map the limits to which, in the modern period . . . the text as a writer's initial choice or intention can be forced" into the mode of self-reflexive narration.[1] After taking a brief look at the questions raised by Henry Adams about the form of his *Education*, we will see in the chapter which follows how, as Said further notes, the self-reflexive work becomes a kind of "obstacle course."[2]

1. Edward W. Said, *Beginnings: Intention and Method* (Baltimore: Johns Hopkins University Press, 1975), 249.
2. Ibid.

Joyce and Proust: The Theory of Fictional Autobiography

The narrative strategy underlying the recuperative and enabling hopes of *Portrait*'s author is, as we have seen, in essence
a revisionary one. As such, Joyce's strategy does bear a relationship to the revisionary poetics of *The Prelude*. But Joyce's fictionalizing is thoroughly pervasive, constituting a much more
purposeful and systematic—a willful—refashioning of the past
into a re-imagined aesthetic pattern, or "portrait." Joyce's work
takes more seriously and self-consciously the Carlylean notion
that the artist's "Condition" is "but the stuff" he "shapes" by
his self-reflexive art—even if its form be "heroic" or "poetic."
Thus, *Portrait* becomes, finally, a Carlylean "History of the man
and his spiritual Endeavour," "forged" in the "lineaments . . .
of Fiction." In its fashion, it turns the Augustinian reliance on
the divine into a reliance on the artistic, and it turns the ostensible Wordsworthian dependence on memory into a dependence
on *willful*, creative revision.[3]

In so doing, Joyce seeks to create a text that is *unhistorical*
in the traditional sense and yet "historical" in what we earlier
saw to be the Nietzchean, aesthetic, sense. *Portrait* presents a
past imaginatively revised not because, like Wordsworth, Joyce
was *unable* to avoid forgetting, but because he was actively and
purposefully *trying* to forget. Thus, *Portrait*'s fictionality becomes the aesthetic counterpart of its protagonist's desire to
forget his past. While Wordsworth's idea is to "faithfully picture"
his "History" because he deems his essential self (and his artistic
power) to reside there, Joyce's idea is to fictionalize his history

---

3. The difference between Wordsworth and Joyce in this regard, it should
be reiterated, is that while both *The Prelude* and *Portrait* present created,
re-imagined, and thus partly fictional protagonists, Joyce willfully and systematically does so while Wordsworth does so only insofar as he cannot avoid
representing his "Wordsworth" as a fictional creation. Stephen Dedalus is
patently and purposefully a fictional character, but "Wordsworth" is a fictional
character in spite of the poet's best efforts to render his own history "as it was."

because he deems *his* essential self (and his artistic power) to be dependent on the very creative process that is to "forge" them. Since his past is not to be "recovered" but overcome, it is forgotten in and by the act of creating another, imaginary, one. Joyce builds this idea into the developing consciousness of his autobiographical protagonist by way of Stephen's insistent need to move beyond both his personal and his national pasts.

Stephen's malady is precisely the one focused on by Nietzsche in *The Use and Abuse of History*: "the malady of history" (69). Nietzsche insists that man, seeing the past as fixed and unchangeable, encounters history as a burden and a "disease" (70)—something which is both "dead" and threatening to become "the gravedigger of the present" (7). This is just the experience of the past that informs Stephen's need for "flight"; the rigid and threatening burden of a familial, Catholic, and Irish history that, diseased and dying, threatens to become his own gravedigger. Thus "history," in that most famous of phrases from *Ulysses*, is a "nightmare" from which Stephen is "trying to awake."[4] Nietzsche offers in place of man who would be "historical" what he calls "unhistorical man," a man who would *know* the past but have "the power, the art, of *forgetting*" it (69). Nietzsche's categories of "historical" and "unhistorical" form the two poles between which Joyce's protagonist moves in *Portrait*. This movement is metaphorized in *Portrait* in Stephen's repeated feeling that his past self has died, first at Clongowes and later as he visits Cork with his father.[5] At Cork, his "death" at Clongowes is remembered as the beginning of a continuous "fading out" of his previous existence:

> The memory of his childhood suddenly grew dim . . . He had been lost or had wandered out of existence for he no longer

4. Joyce, *Ulysses* (New York: Random House, 1961), 34.
5. The Clongowes scene is on pp. 26–27 of *Portrait*. This is where Stephen, ill in the infirmary, identifies in his suffering with the dead Parnell. Brother Michael's imagined intonation, "He is dead. We saw him upon the catafalque," marks Stephen's imagined death as it marks Parnell's.

existed. How strange to think of him passing out of existence . . .
being lost and forgotten. [92–93]

This image is extended to the famous "conversion" scene on
the beach in Part 4, where Joyce speaks of Stephen's "soul" as
arising "from the grave of boyhood, spurning his graveclothes"
(170). This image of rising prepares us for Stephen's emphatic
assertion later that he must "fly by" the nets of his own history.

The experience of Joyce's protagonist as it is presented in
Portrait helps make it clear why his autobiographical text cannot
depend on memory alone, but must, rather, rely on the transforming power of fictional art. Moreover, Stephen's "death" in
Portrait represents, for Joyce, an experience that is *continuous*
with the book's writing, since he is in part killing off his past as
he creates another pattern for it. If *Portrait* is autobiographical,
it is autobiographical in just this way: Joyce's creation of Stephen
represents a putting to death of his own past and his own past
self, and yet at the same time it represents his rebirth as an
artist. Joyce's "dying" into his own autobiographical text is mirrored by Proust's insistence in *A la recherche* that "Marcel"
"should be able to die once" he has been born into his own
book:

> And then a new light, less dazzling, no doubt, than that other
> illumination which had made me perceive that the work of art
> was the sole means of rediscovering Lost Time, shone suddenly
> within me. And I understood that all these materials for a work
> of literature were simply my past life; I understood that they
> had come to me, in frivolous pleasures, in idleness, in affection,
> in unhappiness, and that I had laid them up in store without
> divining the purpose for which they were destined or even their
> continued existence any more than a seed does when it forms
> within itself a reserve of all the nutritious substances from which
> it will feed a plant. Like the seed, I should be able to die once
> the plant had developed and I began to perceive that I had lived
> for the sake of the plant without knowing it, without ever real-
> izing that my life needed to come into contact with those books
> which I had wanted to write and for which, when in the past I

had sat down at my table to begin, I had been unable to find a subject. And thus my whole life up to the present day might and yet might not have been summed up under the title: A Vocation.[6]

Recognizing here that the "material" for his work as a writer exists in his own "past life," Marcel also recognizes that the kind of "contact" he must make with his projected book will, paradoxically, be deadly. This death, of course, is a necessary prelude to his rebirth *in* his work of art. For Marcel to rediscover "Lost Time" in this way is to discover writing as a self-creative, potentially "redemptive" process, but only in the sense that the work of art subsumes the writer, translating his transitory actual existence into what Marcel calls the "eternal life" of his work of art (264). "The cruel law of art," Proust writes, is that the writer dies "after exhausting every form of suffering" (264). The irony here is that while the work of art becomes like a funerary monument, it memorializes an Other. "Over our head," Proust continues, "grow[s] the grass not of oblivion but of eternal life, the vigorous and luxuriant growth of a true work of art" (264).

This is why Marcel, fearing he may literally be dying just when he has discovered his vocation as a writer, sees death as "a threat not to myself but to my book" (264). Marcel's own self-reflexive text will constitute his attempt—like Joyce's in *Portrait*—to "liberate" a "true self which seemed . . . to be dead, but was not altogether dead" (134). The liberation of the "dead" other is the other side of Marcel's necessary dying into the work he must create, and it is the creation, and completion, of *this* work that is threatened by his own mortality. Thus, death has a kind of sacrificial value for Marcel's work, but that value creates a paradox: death is a necessary and cherished achievement but it is also a central threat *to* that achievement.

6. Marcel Proust, *The Past Recaptured*, trans. Andreas Mayor (New York: Vintage, 1971), 154–55. All further references appear in parentheses in the text.

This is why, at the end of Proust's long work, Marcel is in the curious position of worrying that he might not finish dying into his narrative before he actually dies (a predicament made more richly complex because Proust himself was dying as he wrote Marcel's worry into his text). Thus, by the end of Proust's novel, the attachment between self and work is figured as both complete and precarious. The work of "rediscovering" lost time "was," Proust writes, "my life, was in fact me," but "I was compelled so long as I was alive to keep it attached to me . . . it supported me and . . . perched on its giddy summit I could not myself make a movement without displacing it" (271–72).

Proust, then, makes explicit what remains implicit in Joyce's strategy as he composes *Portrait*: that the writer suffers a liberating kind of "death" as he transforms his past into fictional narrative. For both writers, the autobiographical novel is a kind of burial place, a place in which the past is laid to rest in the very act of giving it new life in a fictional form. The words linked in this formula are "death" and "fiction," but their linkage is mediated by a third word, "forgetting." The fictional text cannot represent the death of the past unless there is implicit in that fictionalizing a willful forgetting of the past. This "forgetting," of course, is of a kind with Nietzsche's conception of that necessary, willful, forgetting that precedes the equally willful act of overcoming the "malady" of history by recreating it artistically. Nietzsche, we must remember, describes this "forgetting" as both a "power" *and* an "art." It is of course paradoxical that forgetting should come to have such an important place in texts usually thought to be based on remembering. But this is precisely the mark of their modernity, of their (aesthetic and epistemological) differences from such precursor texts as Augustine's *Confessions* and Wordsworth's *Prelude*.

In an essay that challenges the primacy of memory in *A la recherche* by insisting that we recognize how forgetting consistently forms the pretext for what Marcel ostensibly simply remembers, Jerry Flieger argues that "Proust's *oeuvre* is less a work of memory than a play of forgetfulness."[7] Note the emphasis in this observation on "play," on the imagination's role in "remembering" once consciousness has been set free by a beneficent forgetting. Understanding Marcel's "forgetfulness" as a "symptom" of his "artistic frame of mind,"[8] Flieger identifies a double function for forgetting in Proust's text. Marcel "remembers" the past only at the expense of forgetting the present moment, and Proust himself "remembers" the past only as far as he forgets his actual past so as to create it imaginatively: "Excused from 'real life,' Proust becomes Marcel. Freed to take liberties with autobiographical fact, he is at liberty to forget the 'real story': his history becomes his *histoire*."[9] If we substitute "Joyce" in the above passage for "Proust" and "Stephen" for "Marcel," we can see that this operation also describes the one that underlies *Portrait*. Proust's text simply works out the *theory* of such an operation.

When Proust has Marcel formulate the act of mind that forms the creative foundation for a work like *A la recherche*, he describes "memory" less as a pure source of illumination than as an enabling context, a prelude to insights generated by the imagination in the present. Marcel's involuntary memory creates a special moment, but the renewal attending that moment is special precisely because it depends on the *histoire* he creates in it. Memory, for Marcel, functions not as it might for a more traditional autobiographer but as it does for a poet. Thus, the "air" he breathes during his moments of "renewal" is the "purer air which the poets have vainly tried to situate in paradise," an air that can only be the vehicle for renewal "if it had been breathed before, since the true paradises are the paradises that we have lost" (132). The key word here is "lost." The paradise of the past necessarily animates Marcel's journey toward a kind

7. Jerry Aline Flieger, "Proust, Freud, and the Art of Forgetting," in *Sub-Stance* 29 (1981), 66.
8. Ibid., 68.
9. Ibid., 67.

of recovery, but the paradise is a paradise always already lost to begin with: "owing to the work of oblivion," Proust writes, the "memory can throw no bridge, form no connecting link" to the past, and it thus "remains in the context of its own place and date," in "isolation" from the present (132). Loss, oblivion, isolation; these are the words that describe Marcel's relationship to his past. They posit memory not as the *source* of insight and renewal but as the point of departure leading toward their creation in the artist's own imagination. With this operation as the key to the efficacy of his autobiographical act, the text cannot, must not, avoid becoming a *fictional* history.

Paralleling this concept of "remembering" creatively in Proust's novel is the idea that the self-reflexive writer performs an interpretive act. Thus, the "sensations" experienced by Marcel in his moments of illumination are described as "signs" that he must "interpret" (138). If the subject experiences in these moments a "reawakening," this is not to say that it is dependent on his remembering a *previous* one. It is, in fact, dependent on a creative re-reading of the past, since past events have "concealed within them not a sensation dating from an earlier time, but a new truth" (138). This "new truth" does not come from the past as such, but must be read and interpreted from what Marcel calls "signs" written in a "magical scrawl" (139). Reading this "inner book of unknown sumbols" is, for Marcel, "an act of creation" (139).[10]

Proust's autobiographical art, then, is not based simply on memory, but on a complex creative act that turns simultaneously on forgetting, interpreting, and fictionalizing. Since it is not solely dependent on involuntary memory and its transcription, Proust's text becomes an arduous labor linked to the kind of "work" outlined in Carlyle's *Sartor*. As Joyce did in composing his "portrait," Proust creates in *A la recherche* a patchwork

10. For an extended discussion of the central role of the decipherment of signs in Proust's search, see Gilles Deleuze, *Proust and Signs*, trans. Richard Howard (New York: George Braziller, 1972).

protagonist, one who is part fact and yet supremely fictional—
an autobiographical figure whose privileged status is based
upon its fictionality. In these two works, all the pitfalls that
Wordsworth encountered have actually become resources. If
the former self in each of them has undergone a kind of "conversion"—as both writers, of course, insist—that conversion is
to be located not in the past moments which they fictionalize
but in the present moments during which they create those
fictions. Thus, the *work* of the self-reflexive artist has an importance that transcends the importance of the *finished* work.

As we noted earlier, this work has its analog in the psychoanalytic process. Freud recognized that the subject's cure
depended less upon his reproduction of actual, verifiable, "real"
occurrences, than on his ability to work with "memories" which
are in fact "products of the imagination . . . intended to serve
as some kind of symbolic representation." Freud also understood that this same principle could be a resource for the writer.
"Incomplete and dim memories of the past," he writes in *Moses
and Monotheism*, "are a great incentive to the artist, for he
is free to fill in the gaps according to the behests of his imagination."[11] If Proust and Joyce (as well as Wordsworth) come round
each in his own way to recognize his autobiographical practice
as, in part, a recuperative exercise, each works with the kind of
freedom recognized by Freud. But, as we saw in Wordsworth's
case, this freedom has its darker side: it can foster a self-analysis
that becomes interminable. It is not too difficult to see how an
autobiographical practice like Proust's, for instance, based as it
is on imaginative creation and intra-subjective interpretation,
could turn into an interminable labor. In fact, this is precisely
what happened. From 1895 on, Proust was almost always at
work on his fictional autobiography, first in the form of his early
Jean Santeuil and later in the form of the massive *A la recherche*. He began the latter in 1909 and continuously expanded

11. Freud, *Moses and Monotheism*, in *Standard Edition*, 23:71.

and revised it until his death in 1922. Even his projected critical essay *Contre Sainte-Beuve*, as Roger Shattuck has observed, "kept turning into personal narrative."[12] Together, these works represent one continuous effort by Proust to find a style and a structure adequate to a treatment of his own growth and development as a writer. This suggests that the value for Proust of *Jean Santeuil* and *A la recherche* lay in part in the self-reflexive analytical work they generated for him.[13]

The interminable nature of Proust's work is mirrored by Joyce's. We have already seen how Joyce's autobiographical project extended itself for ten years, from the short "Portrait" essay of 1904 through two very different novels. Joyce recognized that the length of time he spent on *Stephen Hero* and *Portrait* resulted not so much from aesthetic and technical problems but from his being engaged in a kind of extended purgation. "It would be easy for me to do short novels," he wrote to his brother Stanislaus while composing *Stephen Hero*, but "what I want to wear away in this novel cannot be worn away except by constant dropping."[14] The idea that in writing his autobiographical novel he was engaged in wearing something away is resonant with much of what we have seen to be at the heart of Joyce's conception of his work, for it suggests that the composition or rewriting of a text will somehow erase the past, exhaust it, kill it off. Since this wearing away is also the act of transforming the past into a fiction, there is a way in which this transformation

12. Roger Shattuck, *Marcel Proust* (New York: Viking, 1974), 15.

13. Paralleling this creative "hope" is a necessary and enabling kind of suffering. In *The Past Recaptured*, Marcel insists that "one is afraid of each new literary undertaking because one thinks of the pain one will first have to endure in order to imagine it" (162). Not only must one "suffer in order to apprehend truths," he continues, one must suffer *while* one writes. Thus, when a writer "embarks upon a long labor" he "need have no anxieties" about his capacity to continue to suffer: "Let his intellect begin the work and as he proceeds he will meet with griefs, enough or more than enough . . . to finish it" (162).

14. Joyce, *Selected Letters of James Joyce*, ed. Richard Ellmann (New York: Viking, 1975), 56.

extends itself into his later work, from *Ulysses* through *Finnegans Wake*. Both works register Joyce's preoccupation with autobiographical fiction as an analytically valuable practice, and at the same time an unavoidably interminable one. By retaining Stephen for *Ulysses* (and by projecting much of himself into Bloom) and by creating the autobiographical Shem in *Finnegans Wake*, Joyce evolved a less explicit way than did Proust to continue pursuing the mystery of himself.[15]

Both Joyce and Proust, then, ground their autobiographical works in a Nietzschean realization that effective history is dramatic history, that the past in fact gains its coherence and power in the moments of its construction by the writer's creative vision, from the synthetic power of imagination. In this way the unity and wholeness characteristic of both the novels themselves and their autobiographical subjects reflects an aesthetic, not a remembered, unity and wholeness. The historical subjects in

15. Joyce of course continues to write about himself in *Ulysses* partly by weaving elements of himself into Bloom and Stephen and partly by weaving incidents, people, and places from his life in Dublin into the fabric of his novel. In this sense *Ulysses* is inextricably tied to its author's biography. The difficulty of *Finnegans Wake* can obscure *its* dependence on its author's biography. The Shem chapter of *Finnegans Wake* is, as Bernard Benstock points out, "a mine of information about Joyce himself" (*Joyce-Again's Wake: An Analysis of Finnegans Wake* [Seattle: University of Washington Press, 1965], 223). More importantly, as Benstock also notes, with Shem "Joyce is attempting once again to deal personally as well as objectively with the real problem [of] his own life" (220). In this regard, Benstock sees Shem as "a continuation of the Dedalus figure and a burlesque of him" (216). The idea that Shem provides Joyce with an autobiographical figure with which to pursue problems begun with Stephen in *Portrait* is echoed by Adaline Glasheen, who observes that "Shem is certainly Joyce himself, or rather he is Stephen Dedalus. Joyce satirized the Artist in Stephen, he burlesques him in Shem the Penman" (*A Census of Finnegans Wake: An Index of the Characters and Their Roles* [Evanston: Northwestern University Press, 1956], 119), and by Robert Boyle, who writes that "Joyce's development of his notion of the artist is partially portrayed in Stephen Dedalus, but it achieves its full flowering only in Shem" ("Portrait of the Artist as Balzacian Wilde Ass" in *A Conceptual Guide to Finnegans Wake*, eds. Michael H. Begnal and Fritz Senn [University Park: Pennsylvania State University Press, 1974], 71).

Joyce's and Proust's works are made to embody a truth that is quite consciously created and not recaptured; and in so doing both novelists assimilate into the very texture of their auto-biographical works an epistemological point of view made philo-sophically clear by Carlyle and Nietzsche: that both the psycho-logical self and the literary subject are human constructions is one of the primary methodological premises of both *Portrait* and *A la recherche*. That imagining is privileged over remem-bering in these works constitutes their dramatic and literary realization of a changing epistemology of the subject. In reflect-ing Nietzsche's conception of dramatic history, both novels seek to avoid the kind of chaos Carlyle's *Sartor Resartus* loosed upon the world of literary self-representation.

However, that these works sidestep *Sartor*ian chaos also sig-nals how conservative are their formal innovations over more traditional autobiographical modes. For while their overtly fictionalized forms distance *Portrait* and *A la recherche* from the more rigorously historical approaches of an Augustine or a Wordsworth, as *narratives* they are inextricably linked to these precursors. The ontological status of the subject in these works may in part reflect the epistemological shift we have been tracing through the nineteenth century, but their reliance on chronology, biography, and the form of narrative recall the formal principles that always marked autobiographical works seeking to be life-histories. Thus, although Joyce and Proust acknowledge the imaginatively constructed nature of their auto-biographical subjects, and in so doing foreground the inherent disjunction between a writer and such a subject, they neverthe-less retain by their use of narrative the vision of the self as a unified and whole metaphysical essence which Carlyle and Nietzsche sought to deconstruct. While Carlyle's critiques of subjectivity and narrative self-reflection are embodied in the fictional nature of *Portrait* and *A la recherche*, the recourse to narrative they exhibit avoids the formal destabilizations effected by *Sartor Resartus*, and so separates them from Carlyle's critique. Such a destabilization as we see in *Sartor* never really asserts itself in Joyce's or Proust's narratives; rather, it comes later, in works like those of Valéry, Eliot, and Barthes to be discussed in the following chapter.

The Education of Henry Adams: Multiplicity, Chaos, and the Self-Reflexive Experiment

[H]e used to say, half in jest, that his great ambition was to complete St. Augustine's *Confessions*, but that St. Augustine . . . had worked from multiplicity to unity, while he . . . had to reverse the method and work back from unity to multiplicity.
                                                    —Henry Adams[16]

While Joyce and Proust were busy conceiving their fictional autobiographies, Henry Adams was also grappling with the form, but in ways that look more explicitly ahead to the undoing of its narrative structure.[17] Adams's *Education* appears to be a relatively traditional autobiography and, as such, superficially seems committed to a more or less objective rendering of past experience in chronological order. However, this traditional surface is partly disturbed by its third-person narration, which sustains a highly ironic perspective. This, together with the book's status as both history and philosophy, has led one of Adams's principal critics, Ernest Samuels, to call *The Education* an "autobiographical-philosophical romance."[18] Adams was acutely concerned, as we shall see, with the aesthetic nature of

16. Henry Adams, *The Education of Henry Adams*, ed. Ernest Samuels (Boston: Houghton Mifflin, 1973), pp. xxvii–xxviii. This passage is from the preface which appears over the name of Henry Cabot Lodge, but it was actually composed by Adams. See n. 13, p. 541, *The Education*.

17. Adams probably began *The Education* in late spring 1902, wrote the bulk of it in 1904 and 1905, and finished it early in 1906. See Ernest Samuels, *Henry Adams: The Major Phase* (Cambridge: Harvard University Press, 1964), 255, 330.

18. Samuels, *Henry Adams: The Major Phase*, 359.

his autobiographical enterprise and was well aware that in his "Adams" he was creating, as Samuels observes, a "partially fictive character."[19] But Adams's aesthetic concerns, especially as they are reflected in his letters, have little to do with *The Education*'s problematical status as partly fictionalized fact. They have to do, rather, with an even larger and more troubling concern—the possibility that the form of narrative itself may, finally, be unable to carry the burden of the kind of self-reflexive work he wants to produce. It is in this respect that, with his *Education*, Adams further complicates an already complicated literary problematic. He participates less explicitly in the composition of fictional autobiography than do his Irish and French contemporaries, but at the same time he calls more radically into question both the efficacy of narrative itself as a form for self-reflexive writing and the nature of the ego it is to represent. *The Education* may be an effort to "complete St. Augustine's *Confessions*," but in the attempt Adams ends up looking forward to a self-consciously fragmented and discursive self-reflexive form that will evolve in myriad ways after him.

Although Adams was probably exaggerating a bit when he wrote to William James in February 1908 that *The Education* "interests me chiefly as a literary experiment," the observation is an important one, and it is elaborated in comments that appear throughout his letters.[20] Adams's "experiment" took place under the shadows of two precursors: St. Augustine and Thomas Carlyle. It is no wonder, then, that *The Education* is at once the chronology of a spiritual education and, at the same time, the ironic representation of a fragmented, divided Teufelsdrockhean wanderer. Adams's observation that in composing his *Education* he wanted to "complete" Augustine's *Confessions*, that he aspired "to be bound up with" him,[21] stemmed from his conviction that, of all earlier autobiographers, "St. Augustine alone has an

19. Ibid., 354.
20. For some selections, see *The Education*, 511.
21. Ibid., 514.

idea of literary form,—a notion of writing a story with an end
and object . . . like a romance."[22] A romance, of course, is a
narrative, and what interested Adams about the *Confessions*
was its attempt to narrativize a life in a way that was both
compelling and aesthetically pleasing. But the education Adams
received in writing his *Education* involved, in part, his realizing
that in his own time such an achievement was impossible: "I
have worked ten years to satisfy myself that the thing cannot be
done today . . . I can see where the form fails, but I cannot
see how to correct the failures."[23]

Adams, in fact, projects the lineaments of his own failure
back onto Augustine, so that the *Confessions* become linked to
The Education in a negative way: if Adams's book "completes"
the *Confessions*, it does so by by duplicating the form of its
structural failure. In a letter to Barrett Wendell in March 1909,
Adams, referring to both Augustine and Rousseau, insists

> We have all three undertaken to do what cannot be successfully
> done—mix narrative and didactic purpose and style. The charm
> of the effort is not in winning the game but in playing it. We
> all enjoy the failure. St. Augustine's narrative subsides at last
> into the dry sands of metaphysical theology . . . And I found
> that a narrative style was so incompatible with a didactic or
> scientific style, that I had to write a long supplementary chapter
> to explain in scientific terms what I could not put into narration
> without ruining the narrative.[24]

Adam's "failure" to produce structurally the *kind* of autobiographical text he wanted stemmed from his need to put into it
more than a simple recounting of his protagonist's "experience."
The text he wanted to produce needed a "didactic" and a "scientific" style as well as a narrative one. Like Augustine in the last
four books of his *Confessions*, Adams had to write a "long sup-

22. Ibid., 511.
23. Ibid., 511–12.
24. Ibid., 514.

plementary chapter" in order to incorporate into his work material he deemed necessary but that would not lend itself to the
book's narrative style. It was a game he was charmed to play,
but which he found he could not win.

This stylistic problem is complemented in *The Education* by
an epistemological one. As the stylistic problem links his text
with Augustine's, the epistemological one links it with Carlyle's
Sartor. Carlyle's book, as Samuels has observed, had a "pervasive influence" on *The Education*.[25] Adams tips his hat to
Carlyle in the 1907 Preface to *The Education*:

> Since [Rousseau's] time, and largely thanks to him, the Ego has
> steadily tended to efface itself, and, for purposes of model, to
> become a manikin on which the toilet of education is to be
> draped in order to show the fit or misfit of the clothes. The
> object of study is the garment, not the figure. The tailor adapts
> the manikin as well as the clothes to his patron's wants.[26]

The Carlylean link in *The Education* is a double one: the protagonist of Adam's book is a "new Teufelsdrockh" (*The Education*,
414), a "wanderer," *and* he is less a coherent, whole individual
than a patchwork of selves both past and present, literal and
figurative. What Adams shares with Carlyle, as Samuels puts it,
is that he sees "the essential naiveté of the romantic conception
of the ego as a unitary, indestructible and unchanging self,"
understanding that "personality was more like a council of anarchists."[27] As in *Sartor*, the patchwork ego in *The Education*
also reflects the status of the writer as a tailor: Adams's manikin,
as one critic puts it, grows into the "artful tailor," the artist.[28]

Adams resists Carlyle's way of translating the problematical
nature of subjectivity into the very structure of his work, but

25. *The Education*, 542. For more on the influence of Carlyle on *The Education* see Samuels, *Henry Adams: The Major Phase*, 347–53.

26. *The Education*, xxx.

27. Samuels, *Henry Adams: The Major Phase*, 347.

28. Robert F. Sayre, *The Examined Self: Benjamin Franklin, Henry Adams,
Henry James* (Princeton: Princeton University Press, 1964), 109.

he does thematize it. This thematization is part of *The Education*'s general tendency to run from comfortable order to uncomfortable chaos, whether it is talking about the state of "history," "science," *or* the subject.[29] "From cradle to grave," Adams writes, "this problem of running order through chaos . . . unity through multiplicity, has always been . . . the task of education" (12). The original title of his book—*The Education of Henry Adams: A Study in Twentieth-Century Multiplicity*—was meant to emphasize at the outset the trajectory of his education. This "multiplicity" signifies, in part, Adams's conception of the subject. His own "identity" is called "a bundle of disconnected memories" (209). His "self" is described at one point as "a conscious ball of vibrating motions" (460), and he refers to himself throughout *The Education* as being "broken into separate pieces" (209) or into "halves" (294). Complementing this conception of a broken, fragmented ego is Adams's tendency to generate a number of figurative identities for himself in *The Education*: he is an "18th-century boy," a "begonia," an historian, a statesman, a man of letters, and so on. He also links himself to a variety of literary figures—Adam, Odysseus, Rasselas, Teufelsdrockh, Faust, Hamlet, Augustine, Dante, Shakespeare, and Gibbon, among them.

Adams's book, finally, is not only the autobiography of "Adams"; it is also a kind of case history of the emergence of modernism. Because he saw history, science, subjectivity, and the literary *forms* of both historiography and autobiography

29. Adams's book views historical progression as a "snapped continuity" (457). It does so in part because Adams came to believe that history followed the laws of nature, and that "Chaos was the law of nature" (451). During this period in his life, he began to see Entropy everywhere, a process of "degradation" he took to be more than just a metaphor of social and cultural—as well as epistemological—erosion. See also Henry Adams, *The Degradation of the Democratic Dogma* (New York: Peter Smith, 1949). For a discussion of Adams's views on historical progression in this regard, see my "American Modernism and the Uses of History: The Case of William Carlos Williams," in *New Orleans Review* 9:3 (Winter 1982), 17–20.

as running toward multiplicity and chaos, Adams was led to observe that the "experiment" of his book was "hazardous . . . as art."[30] When he wrote that he had to "reverse the method" of Augustine, "and work back from unity to multiplicity," he was linking the book's underlying conception of subjectivity with the "failure" of its method. If the subject was now to be perceived as multiple, changing, and chaotic, then the narrative form of autobiography was also heading toward the kind of chaos Carlyle had already embodied in *Sartor*. Augustine's *Confessions* could move methodically from multiplicity to unity because it had an epistemological and a literary reason for doing so. Augustine's subject had, he believed, its source in a unity which it could return to, and his confession was meant to tell the truth of his life to an all-knowing God. This epistemological ground had, of course, crumbled under Adams, and he thus found his process of composition reversed. With intuitions of chaos all around him, it is no wonder that he finds "after sixty or seventy years of growing astonishment," that his mind has awakened "to find itself looking blankly into the void of death" (460).

If writing *The Education* was the process of *gaining* an education—and there is ample evidence in the letters that this was Adams's view (among other things it educated him "in the possibilities of literary form," and in the possibilities of its failure[31]), it was also conceived as a putting to death of its author. In a number of letters Adams refers to his project as a way to take his own life, to "go to sleep."[32] To Charles Gaskell he wrote that *The Education* was his "last Will and Testament,"[33] and to Henry James he suggested that it was a beneficent form of suicide: "The volume is a mere shield of protection in the grave.

---

30. *The Education*, 513.
31. See the letters on pp. 510, 511, 512 and 515 of *The Education*.
32. Ibid., 509.
33. Ibid., 508.

I advise you to take your own life in the same way."[34] Here Adams seizes upon a metaphor already familiar from Joyce and Proust. His strategy for putting his past to death by putting it into his self-reflexive text is every bit as ambitious as theirs, and it is a strategy that seeks recourse to a more complex and complicated textual operation. While Joyce and Proust move autobiography squarely into the realm of fiction, Adams seeks a technique at once less explicitly *creative* and yet in its way more daring than theirs, since he attempts to be in part fictional and in part factual, blending narrative, historiography, political commentary, and scientific theory into a form of "multiplicities" that reflects the multiplicity of its own subject.

If Adams's book is insistently about the end—the end of history, the end of historiography, the end of the "whole" and "coherent" ego, and the end of "Adams"—it is also about the ends to which autobiography, as a *narrative* practice, has come. His observations about the real limitations of narrative as a form for the twentieth-century self-reflexive writer are tied to the *expanding* limits of humankind's conception of the self. Adams's text reveals the ways in which the latter had come to outgrow the former. His interest in multiplicity, coupled with the disparate forms of his autobiographical text, looks forward to twentieth-century self-reflexive strategies that thematize the literary and psychological subjects as philosophical problems and seek non-narrative, discursive forms with which to do so. As I will show in my final chapter, such works recall the Carlylean and Nietzschean critiques of the subject that we reviewed earlier. Grounded as they are in such critiques, these works provide clear evidence of the autobiographical writer's continuing response to epistemological dislocations dating from the nine-

---

34. Ibid., 512–13. For a discussion of *The Education* as a "strategy for suicide," see Mutlu Konuk Blasing, *The Art of Life: Studies in American Autobiographical Literature* (Austin: University of Texas Press, 1977), 90–94.

teenth century. Autobiographical fiction of course continues in the wake of Joyce and Proust. But alongside such narratives grow counter-strategies for literary self-representation that consciously abandon and undercut the central premises of narrative self-history whether factual or fictional.

CHAPTER SIX

A Strange Mimesis: The Discourse of Fragmentation

He more or less remembers the order in which he wrote these fragments; but where did that order come from? In the course of what classification, of what succession? He no longer remembers. The alphabetical order [of *Roland Barthes*] erases everything, banishes every origin. Perhaps in places, certain fragments seem to follow one another by some affinity; but the important thing is that these little networks not be connected, that they not slide into a single enormous network which would be the structure of the book, its meaning. It is [written] in order to halt, to deflect, to divide this descent of discourse toward a destiny of the subject . . .

—Roland Barthes, *Roland Barthes*

Adams's declaration that in his autobiography he had to "reverse the method" of Augustine's *Confessions* by working "back from unity to multiplicity" emphasizes how thoroughly the strategies appropriate to that ancient text were mediated during the nineteenth century by a philosophical critique of the self. We have seen that from Wordsworth on, changing ideas about the nature of subjectivity and its literary representation have been reflected in changing approaches to the very form of self-reflexive literature. Wordsworth's acknowledgment in *The Prelude* that there was a "wide vacancy" between himself and the protagonist of his poem and that language was a "frail element" to use as its representation presaged an evolving epistemological problem that was to have an impact on the very form of literary self-representation. These two problems emerge in parallel fashion in *Sartor Resartus* and are engaged in differing ways by Joyce, Proust, and Adams. Joyce and Proust tend to ignore the *mis en abyme* between author and subject by taking up an overtly fictional form; Adams weaves this *mis en abyme* into his text as one of its subjects and in so doing discovers the "frailty" of narrative itself.

Doubts like Adams's—about the efficacy of narrative as a vehicle for self-reflexive representation and about the unity and cohesiveness of the psychological subject—surface in a number of modern self-reflexive texts. There, these doubts vie with the history of the autobiographical subject for thematic prominence. In such works, the psychoanalytic function that we observed in Wordsworth's poem gives way to a more abstract philosophical analysis of the self. In closing this study with brief looks at Paul Valéry's *Cahiers*, T. S. Eliot's *Four Quartets*, and Roland Barthes's *Roland Barthes*, I pursue the "destiny of the subject" in self-reflexive texts where narrativity is virtually abandoned for discursiveness and where preoccupations are more philosophical and deconstructive than psychological and therapeutic. In so doing these texts align themselves with the kind of philosophical self-consciousness we have already observed in varying degrees in Wordsworth, Carlyle, Proust, and Adams. *Cahiers, Four Quartets,* and *Roland Barthes* are each "autobiographical," but in all of them *biography* has been displaced as the ostensible subject by an insistent focus on epistemological, psychological, and representational problems. Although in each text, biographical content and narrative form are displaced by philosophical content and discursive form, the subject matter remains inextricably rooted in the self who writes. What we witness in them is an on-going redefinition (and critique) of subjectivity, grounded in the earlier work of thinkers like Carlyle and Nietzsche. If the form of these modern works is fragmented, that is because traditional ideas about subjectivity seem to their authors to demand such a form. Though they seem self-effacing, they are not; the writer's "life" remains central in each, but that "life," and the "self" that experiences it, are no longer deemed constituted by a chronological or historical series of experiences that are—or even should be—narratable. In each the search for self-definition is as insistent as any we encounter in reading Wordsworth (or Augustine); it is just that the definitions we encounter, and the literary forms they take, are both new and curious.[1]

Paul Valéry's *Moi*: Self-Representation as Auto-philosophy

Questions about the nature of the psychological subject and its literary representation form an ongoing discourse in Paul Valéry's *Cahiers*, handwritten notebooks composed between 1894 and his death in 1945, notebooks in which, he writes, his "*moi* most clearly takes shape."[2] While the notebooks are

1. This is not to say, of course, that both autobiography *per se* and fictional autobiography do not persist during this period. In the twentieth century, self-reflexive literary practices have in fact proliferated, and my treatment of discursive, self-conscious strategies should not be taken as an assertion that this is *the* form under which we can group most autobiographical projects in the modern period. As I make clear at the end of this chapter, works like those treated here do not represent a single end to which autobiographical practices have come, but *one* of the ends to which this peculiarly metamorphic form has come. If a history of autobiography could be written, it would not be an account of progress toward a formal end, but one of successive accretions. The three texts with which I have chosen to finish this study have been picked primarily because they extend our meditation on ontological and representational problems into our own time.

2. Paul Valéry, *Moi*, ed., trans. Marthiel and Jackson Mathew (Princeton: Princeton University Press, 1975), 287. The complete *Cahiers* were published in Paris by Centre National de la Recherche Scientifique in 1957.

much more than "autobiography," the theory of self-reflexive representation that they articulate clearly asserts that their discursive form and their wealth of topics are generated partly in order to produce a new and more precise kind of autobiographical text. This is the point of Valéry's Foreword to the only part of the *Cahiers* to be published before his death, a fragment entitled "Propos me concernant" (Remarks About Myself):

> The text of these "Remarks" brings together without order or system a few jottings and fragments from my notebooks, having to do with many things other than the author himself. Could it be that in these remnants his *moi* most clearly takes shape? They are no more than moments caught and set down as they came . . . with the repetitions, the gaps, the fluctuations . . . recorded by the meter of any life . . . I do not keep, I have never kept a record of my days . . . What do I care about my biography? What do my used-up days matter to me? Nothing of the past should be retained but . . . the bounty snatched from time . . . which necessarily loses at the same time its attachment to it source . . . No, I have no fondness for memories, which to me are images already used, a dreary useless waste . . . No, no! It is no pleasure to retrace in my mind those old paths of my life. I am not one to pursue remembrance of things past.[3]

This Foreword does two things; it questions both traditional conceptions about what constitutes the "self" and traditional conceptions about what constitutes the proper representation of that "self" in self-reflexive literature. The reference to Proust foregrounds Valéry's break with the idea that the "self" is what it remembers, and that, therefore, an autobiographical text should be an auto-*biography*. For Valéry the "self" and its "biography" —its "used-up days"—have a discontinuous relationship, so that "memory" does not animate, but necessarily hinders, the author's work. If there is a relationship between the self, writ-

3. Valéry, *Moi*, 287–88. Further references to this work appear in parentheses in the text.

ing, and the past, it is a paradoxical one: the past may be a "source," but it is a "used-up" one, a dry well whose meaning is lost in the obscurity of time. A "truthful" rendering of the past—when the past enters into the work at all—will be fragmented, repetitious, and full of gaps.

While Augustine, Wordsworth, or Proust may distrust the memory for its inaccuracies, Valéry distrusts it quite as much even when it seems to *be* accurate. "Memory," he writes, "is often as deceiving when accurate as when treacherous" (289). Moreover, he insists that "the past . . . is more obliterated for me in its *chronological* and *narratable* development, so it seems to me, than it is for most" (289). The past, that is, exists for Valéry in a specifically nonchronological form, so that the most "treacherous" thing he could do as a writer would be to make it chronological and "narratable." The fragmentary nature of his *Cahiers*, and of the shorter "Remarks," then, is meant to represent the quality of his relationship to his "past" and not to obfuscate it.

The "obliteration" of which Valéry speaks does not so much refer to a past that has disappeared as to a past that has been assimilated by the mind in a way that unavoidably transforms it. His mind retains from the past only what "can be assimilated so intimately that it is no longer the past but an element of potential action, a resource for the future" (290). In this way the past is "obliterated" because it is necessarily lost in the obscurity of time, but this obliteration is a resource for the writer, since the past has become part of the present in which he is writing. It thus constitutes an element of his "potential action" in that present, which is itself a gesture toward "the future." Here Valéry is close to Wordsworth's conception of the past as moments that are "enshrined" in the mind for the poet's "restoration" in the "future."

The relationship envisioned by Valéry between his nonchronological past and his fragmented text is mirrored in the continuity he sees between that text and his own "*moi.*" That is,

perceiving his own "nature" as fragmented and disunited, he
has fashioned his self-reflexive work in a fragmented and disunited fashion (something we observed Carlyle doing in *Sartor
Resartus*). "I find no unity in my nature," he writes. "I see
nothing [there] but a 'result of chance'" (291). A narrative,
which would transform this pattern into a chronological one,
would betray the very texture of the "life" it sought to evoke:

> History can record little else than "events." But reduce a man
> to the facts that are the most striking and the easiest to perceive
> and define—his birth, his few adventures, his death—and you
> have lost sight of the texture of his life. Reduce a life to a "sum-
> mary"! It is just the opposite that might be worth something.
> [291]

Here an autobiographical method involving narration of its author's "history"—the "events" of his life—is understood less as
a representaion than a *reduction*. The "opposite" method, for
Valéry, is an artistic one—formally innovative and fictional by
its very nature. With Nietzsche, Joyce, and Proust, Valéry insists that "the writing of History is an art—nothing less, but
nothing more" (294). However, unlike Joyce and Proust, he
has no interest in binding a self-reflexive art to *narrative*. He
envisions a self-reflexive practice that does not constitute a sum-
mation of the past but an *intervention* in it: "I am aware that,
once my pen intervenes, I can make whatever I like out of
what was" (301–302). A text produced in such a way is based
on the past but in an explicitly creative way—not to relive it
chronologically but to make it new: "Never do I write to relive—
what a weakness" (319).

When compared to the autobiographical projects of Augustine
and Wordsworth, to a traditional conception of autobiography
like that practiced by, say, Benjamin Franklin, or even to the
practices of a thinly disguised "fictional" autobiography like
Joyce's *Portrait*, Valéry's text constitutes a kind of anti-practice.
However, Valéry's method (so far as we can speak of it as a

"method" at all) does not set out to be anti-mimetic but to be mimetic in a new way, a way that seems to him to be more congruent with his sense of self than a biographical narrative could be. Valéry observes a kind of seamlessness between the discontinuous, "chance" components of his "*moi*" and the fragmented form of his work. For him the self is "heaped together" in "successive accretions" of "accidents" from the outside that give it a "certain *shape*," a shape "composed of bits and pieces that have never coexisted" (310). This is, of course, the very shape of his *Cahiers*, and its mimetic relationship to its author is made explicit when Valéry writes that "the entity Mr. P.V." is "a 'convenient notation'" (315).

Since the "*moi*" in "Remarks" is not the biographical Valéry but an aesthetic creation, reading his text gives a sense of an absolute kind of distance between the "remembered" and the writing self, a sense that in the activity of writing Valéry is for the moment creating a "person" to write about another person who does not—did not—exist. We recognize in the work the presence of an ephemeral, and yet an insistent, "other" whom it both animates and sustains. Recognizing this, Valéry writes elsewhere that he "is made up of many different persons and a principal witness who watches all these puppets bobbing."[4] It

4. Valéry, *Moi*, 14. For another discussion of the autobiographical aspects of Valéry's work—this, in regard to his poetry—see James Olney's discussion of Valéry's "La Jeune Parque" in James Olney, ed., *Autobiography: Essays Theoretical and Critical* (Princeton: Princeton University Press, 1980), 249–59. Olney uses his discussion of this poem in part to show how Valéry's conception of "autobiography," can aggravate our "generic sensibilities" (249). Olney points out that Valéry called "La Jeune Parque" "an autobiography," even though it contains no biography, and that he said of his poem "Le cimetière marin" that "it is almost the only one of my poems into which I put something of my own life," and yet he insisted that this poem was *not* an autobiography. Olney's drawing of the obvious paradox here, that "a poem that draws on memory to reconstruct something from the poet's personal past is *not* an autobiography, while a poem that disdains memory altogether and has in it nothing of the poet's personal history *is* an autobiography" (249), reveals the same negative relationship to memory and biography that we have been observing in "Propos me concernant."

is the search to understand this "principal witness" that, he suggests at the close of "Remarks," both animates and troubles any self-reflexive writer:

> What is there of mine in what comes to me? What is there of me in what comes from me? Here the ridiculous problem of inspiration converges with the ridiculous problem of responsibility.
>
> In both cases the self is searching for a self. Who has done what I have done? . . .
>
> One *self* produces and acts; the other receives and sometimes judges.
>
> —But why in the devil do you have to *introduce* this self. And this *introduces* a new question. [332–333]

T. S. Eliot's *Four Quartets*: Retrospection and the Poetry of Deferral

The "other" in Valéry's observation is skeptical self-consciousness—not the self who "produces and acts" but the one who "receives" and "judges." This "witness" oversees the writer's search for a coherent, unified self by probing and questioning that search at its every turn. In "Propos me concernant," this produces a text in which the nature of the subject and the methods of its representation are questioned and redefined. In Eliot's *Four Quartets*, the poet's skepticism is also aimed at the problems inherent in literary self-representation, but in Eliot's case the focus is less on the adequacy or the inadequacy of memory than on the adequacy or inadequacy of language itself. Eliot's poem is a troubled one in the tradition of Wordsworth: its autobiographical meditation is repeatedly disturbed by discursive passages doubting the efficacy of the poet's redemptive project. Its didacticism and its discursivity, that is, are a composite sign of the poet's anxiety about the efficacy of his text, and the "self" that is its subject possesses the kinds of doubts that align its creator more with Wordsworth, Carlyle, and Adams than with Augustine. The destiny of the subject in Eliot's poem is to remain, like that of Wordsworth's, "something evermore about to be."

Although Eliot's poem shares some obvious affinities with the kind of spirtual journey Augustine sought to enact in writing his *Confessions*, it has, as William Spanos has observed, been misunderstood too long as a "poem that, in enacting its circular theme, in achieving closure, recuperates the traditional Christian formal paradigm."[5] Actually, by continually calling into question the very possibility of the recovery it seeks to enact, Eliot's poem tends both to leave open the circle it seeks to close and to discover, if not affirm, the absence of what it is searching for. It does so, of course, by repeatedly observing that its language is unable to achieve the kind of renewal its poet seeks:

> So here I am, in the middle way . . .
>
>   .   .   .
>
> Trying to learn to use words, and every attempt
> Is a wholly new start, and a different kind of failure
> Because one has only learnt to get the better of words
> For the thing one no longer has to say, or the way in which
> One is no longer disposed to say it. And so each venture
> Is a new beginning, a raid on the inarticulate
> With shabby equipment always deteriorating
> In the general mess of imprecision of feeling,
> Undisciplined squads of emotion. And what there is to conquer
> By strength and submission, has already been discovered
> Once or twice, or several times, by men whom one cannot hope
> To emulate—but there is no competition—
> There is only the fight to recover what has been lost
> And found and lost again and again. . . .
>
>   ["East Coker," 5]

5. William V. Spanos, "Hermeneutics and Memory: Destroying T. S. Eliot's *Four Quartets*," in *Genre* 11:4 (Winter 1978), 523. For an extended deconstructive reading of *Four Quartets* see Gregory S. Jay, *T. S. Eliot and the Poetics of Literary History* (Louisiana State University Press, 1983), "Part Four."

The circularity suggested in this passage is hardly that envisioned by Augustine, who, with recourse to the Word, believed he had a divine *place* to return to and a transcended self to become. Rather, it is the circularity of repetition, and it is characterized by worldy struggle: the "fight" here is to "recover what has been lost/And found and lost again and again." The struggle is temporal and repetitive because it is a struggle with language itself, a struggle "to use words" for "the thing one no longer has to say." But belatedness is only part of the problem; Eliot's paradox is the paradox *per se* of any text that seeks to be self-reflexive: the poet's "intolerable wrestle/With words and meanings" is the effort to grasp and articulate a "knowledge derived from experience," but the very language of that articulation "imposes a pattern," and in so doing, "falsifies" ("East Coker," 2). So Eliot's poem, like Marcel's novel, continually becomes a monument to the Other.

As the poet persists in trying to find and articulate himself by writing his poem, its repetitions become a series of new starts. But "every attempt" is a "different kind of failure," another "way of putting it," so that each poem in the sequence becomes a "wholly new start," another repetition in Eliot's struggle with language. What he calls the "fight to recover what has been lost" is his ongoing struggle in the poem to give what is lost a linguistic reality commensurate with his own vision of it. The repetitious nature of this effort is founded on the poet's recognition that "Words strain,/Crack and sometimes break, under the burden,/Under the tension, slip, slide, perish,/Decay with imprecision, will not stay in place,/Will not stay still" ("Burnt Norton," 5). Thus, each poem moves not toward a completion of the poet's effort but toward sustaining his discourse *about* the vicissitudes of that effort. Each poem leads to its successor because each final section articulates a kind of crisis. Each must inaugurate a new start, a new "raid on the inarticulate," that the last has not resolved. "Old men," Eliot writes, "ought to be explorers/Here and there does not matter/

We must be still and still moving/Into another intensity" ("East Coker," 5).

Eliot's specific attempt to move into another "intensity" does recall Augustine's, and his preoccupation with words as the vehicle for that movement reminds us of the importance of the Word in the *Confessions*. But, while "every phrase and every sentence" provides both "an end and a beginning" for Eliot's search ("Little Gidding," 5), the other "intensity" he seeks is an intensity outside of time and hence outside, beyond, the power of *his* words. Thus, the "still point" he seeks slips, slides, and disappears just as do the words he seeks to grasp it with:

> . . . [A]t the still point, there the dance is,
> But neither arrest nor movement. And do not call it fixity,
> Where past and future are gathered. Neither movement from nor
>   towards
> Neither ascent nor decline.
>
>   ["Burnt Norton," 2]

Eliot's speech about this "point" must always be belated, it must always signify something absent, or evermore *about* to be. Like Wordsworth's nostalgia for metaphysical presence, it must always have its home in an infinitude beyond language:

> I can only say, *there* we have been: but I cannot say where.
> And I cannot say, how long, for that is to place it in time.
>   ["Burnt Norton," 2]

If Eliot's search for Presence continually ends by signifying absence, if the poem's speech both differs from that Presence and defers it, this, at least, is a recognition gained by Eliot in its composition. In the final poem of the *Quartets*, "Little Gidding," the "you" to whom it is spoken is in part the poet himself, and the realization is his own:

> . . . [W]hat you thought you came for
> Is only a shell, a husk of meaning

> From which the purpose breaks only when it is fulfilled
> If at all. Either you had no purpose
> Or the purpose is beyond the end you figured
> And is altered in fulfilment.
>
> ["Little Gidding," 1]

What remains for Eliot at the end of the *Quartets* is only the "husk," the outer "shell," of the meaning he came into the poem searching for. The "purpose" of his poem, he has discovered, is "beyond" the purpose he had "figured," and has become "altered in fulfilment." *This* end, of course, is the poet's beginning: "What we call the beginning is often the end/And to make an end is to make a beginning./The end is where we start from" ("Little Gidding," 5). The poem ends not with a declaration of discovery but with a declaration that the poet must continue the "exploration" begun in his poem:

> We shall not cease from exploration
> And the end of all our exploring
> Will be to arrive where we started
> And know the place for the first time.
>
> ["Little Gidding," 5]

If we want to measure Eliot's progress in writing the poem, we can contrast this declaration with the hope which begins it. Early in "Burnt Norton," Eliot declares the "purpose" he has come for: "The inner freedom from the practical desire,/The release from action and suffering" (2). It is this meaning that has disappeared in the course of the poem, leaving only its husk, this "purpose" that lies broken in the end. The new, and contrasting intention—to never cease exploration—affirms "practical desire" and *embraces* both "action" and "suffering."

Four Quartets is a poem concerned with the "use of memory," but its purpose is in part "the liberation" of the poet from his past ("Little Gidding,"3). The poem has an autobiographical base—rooted primarily in the places for which each poem is named—but its relationship to the past is less one of "servitude" than one of "freedom": "See, now they vanish,/The faces and places, with the self which, as it could, loved them/To become renewed, transfigured, in another pattern" ("Little Gidding,"3). Eliot's line is in its way emblematic of any autobiographical act, an act in which the writer's past is always transfigured in *another* pattern, and it contains a measure of pathos as well as a measure of hope: the transfiguration may be liberating but it is also unavoidable, inevitable, a failure of memory as well as an accomplishment of art.[6]

The poem's discursiveness, its repeated preoccupation with philosophical and representational problems, are signs that the destiny of its subject is to explore rather than to discover. The "shabby equipment" of Eliot's words are his best hope, but their temporality keeps the poem weighted down, caught in a kind of time only a saint can escape. This is why Eliot recognizes that his journey can never be the journey charted in Augustine's *Confessions*:

> Men's curiosity searches past and future
> And clings to that dimension. But to apprehend
> The point of intersection of the timeless
> With time, is an occupation for the saint—
>
> .   .   .
>
> For most of us, there is only the unattended
> Moment, the moment in and out of time,
> The distraction fit, lost in a shaft of sunlight,
> The wild thyme unseen . . .
>
> .   .   .
>
> . . . These are only hints and guesses,
> Hints followed by guesses; and the rest
> Is prayer, observance, discipline, thought and action.
>   ["Dry Salvages," 5]

6. For a discussion of *Four Quartets* as a spiritual autobiography, and of its meaning *as* autobiography, see James Olney, *Metaphors of Self: The Meaning of Autobiography* (Princeton: Princeton University Press, 1972), 260–316.

If the poem's prayerful observance and the spiritual nature of its goal recall Augustine, its distractions, losses, hints, and guesses recall the problematic subject in *The Prelude*. But since the poem ends by affirming the explorations of *this* subject, its philosophical and representational tensions are folded into its spiritual and religious ones. The repeated waves of doubt about the efficacy of his language that nearly swamp Eliot's ship (we think of the poet, with the fishermen in "The Dry Salvages," as "forever bailing") lend their drama to the spiritual drama unfolded by the poem, and in this assimilation, the poem's philosophical problems are kept under control, as one drama becomes the other. With Eliot always working in the belief that there may be for the soul a final and timeless moment of "Incarnation," an "impossible union" where "the past and future/Are conquered, and reconciled" ("Dry Salvages," 5), the writer's representational problems are folded into his spiritual ones, so that the difficulties of Eliot's poetic "explorations" become emblems of the difficulties of the spiritual exploration that the poem affirms. In this way, Eliot's belief seems to control the representational problems he confronts in writing his poem. Doubtful though he becomes about his words and about their ability to sustain and redeem him, Eliot's poem never becomes consumed by a conscious intellectual effort to deconstruct the conception of the "self" that informs it.

Roland Barthes's *Roland Barthes*: Disorder and the Destiny of the Subject

In contrast to Eliot's *Four Quartets*, Roland Barthes's *Roland Barthes* is an autobiographical work that seeks to *be* the deconstructed self, and it does so because it wants at every turn to attenuate the *risk* of transcendence."[7] In so doing, Barthes

7. *Roland Barthes by Roland Barthes*, trans. Richard Howard (New York: Hill and Wang, 1977), 95. All further references to this work appear in parentheses in the text.

works methodically in his book to construct a discursive form
that is liberated from the narrative mode required by a nostalgia
for the past. His book, he declares, is "a movement of abolition,
not of truth" (56). Like Valéry, Barthes abolishes both memory
and biography as controlling elements for his self-reflexive text,
and he insists that his autobiographical work is a creative text,
the subject within it a textual production. "I do not," he writes,
"try to *restore* myself . . . I do not say: 'I am going to describe
myself' but: 'I am writing a text, and I call it R. B.' . . . I
am the story which happens to me" (56). Barthes's method for
dealing with the inherent distance between the biographical
and the textual self is to affirm that distance, and so he deconstructs "Roland Barthes" into an alphabetical group of textual
fragments arranged under a series of names, topics, and con-
cepts. The "important thing," he insists,

> is that these little networks not be connected, that they not
> slide into a single enormous network which would be the struc-
> ture of the book . . . It is in order to halt, to deflect, to divide
> this descent of discourse toward a destiny of the subject, that at
> certain moments [the network] calls you to order (to disorder)
> and says: *Cut! Resume the story in another way* . . . [148]

With this fragmented structure Barthes attempts to avoid the
illusory representation of the self as what Nietzsche describes
as "one substratum": with Nietzsche, Barthes's text is a sustained
denial of the fiction that the subject is anything other than a
creation of human consciousness and human language.

Like Valéry's approach to writing autobiographically, Barthes's
constitutes a kind of anti-practice. The "destiny" of Barthes's
subject is just the opposite of Eliot's: if *Four Quartets* remember to re-member, to bring together time and the timeless, to
reconcile, *Roland Barthes* devalues the past in order to create
disorder—to "halt," "deflect," and to "divide" the subject from
its "destiny." The older and too easy conception of the subject
as whole, unified, and spiritual ("a single enormous network")

is understood by Barthes to be grounded not in Nature or in Divinity but rather in a historically constructed idea, a metaphor that we have forgotten *is* a metaphor. Likewise, Barthes is also working in his text to undo the notion that a "self," "whole" and "recovered," can restore itself in, or by writing, a text. Thus, while Augustine wrote his *Confessions* because he "lay in shattered pieces," Barthes writes what is specifically an anti-confession of fragments that he "calls R. B." to demonstrate, in part, that the "self" *is* shattered, scattered, decentered, and—at least in a text—always a "fiction:"

> This book is not a book of "confessions;" not that it is insincere, but because we have a different knowledge today than yesterday; such knowledge can be summarized as follows: What I write about myself is never *the last word*: the more "sincere" I am, the more interpretable I am, under the eye of other examples than those of the old authors, who believed they were required to submit themselves to but one law: *authenticity* . . . my texts are disjointed . . . the latter is nothing but a *further* text . . . *text upon text*, which never illuminates anything. [120]

Here, instead of the Augustinian pilgrim's end—a divinely "authentic" illumination" that redeems the self for a transcendent and eternal end—Barthes is affirming what Eliot called the "exploration" which the use of language itself affords. While this "movement," this exploration, regularly brought Eliot's poem to a point of crisis, for Barthes it is meant to be a sustaining force. For him, the autobiographical writer's movement is through an ever-interpretable self, who has no single "law" with which to designate his "authenticity." There is for Barthes no language that might consitute the last, the redemptive, the incarnate Word—certainly no language about the "past" that will grace the self with enlightenment: "What right does my present have to speak of my past? Has my present some advantage over my past? What grace might have enlightened me?" (121)

Based in part on the denial of such a "grace," Barthes's text seeks to deconstruct—or to reconstruct—the ontological foundations of the autobiographical text.[8] This is why it works so rigorously against being *nostalgic*, why it works, in fact, to present nostalgia as the condition of an illusion. In methodical fashion, it resists nostalgia for the past, nostalgia for a past "self," and nostalgia for a more authentic narrative mode with which to present both. Barthes writes about himself in his book "without . . . ever knowing whether it is about my past or my present that I am speaking" (142). In denying that his past has any advantage over his present, his text rejects nostalgia in favor of the more creative moments in which he is actually composing it. The very negation of "recovery," his "patchwork" text is a rewriting of the self who writes: "I . . . *rewrite* myself—at a distance, a great distance—here and now" (142).

For Barthes, nostalgia constitutes the illusory sense that there is a "place" for the autobiographer to return to, and another self there for him to reanimate. A corollary of the idea that the self can simply be "divided," this notion of a "homesick" self is replaced with a more ghostly image of the subject as "dispersed" and "diffracted" *in the present*. In a fragment under the title "The person divided?" he writes that

> when we speak today of a divided subject, it is never to acknowl-
> edge his simple contradictions, his double postulations, etc.; it
> is a *diffraction* which is intended, a dispersion of energy in
> which there remains neither a central core nor a structure of
> meaning: I am not contradictory, I am dispersed. [143]

8. Barthes realizes, it should be noted, that his own text cannot remain exempt from such a deconstruction. Of *Roland Barthes*, he writes, "I have the illusion to suppose that by breaking up my discourse I cease to discourse in terms of the imaginary about myself, attenuating the risk of transcendence; but since the fragment . . . is *finally* a rhetorical genre and since rhetoric is that layer of language which best presents itself to interpretation, by supposing I disperse myself I merely return, quite docilely, to the bed of the imaginary" (95).

Roland Barthes, written to foreground this idea, resists the lure of both an idealized past *and* the idea that there is an "other" self residing there, so that a prior period of self-unification can never stand as its subject's goal. We need to note here, by point of contrast, how operative is the relationship for both Wordsworth and Augustine between writing a nostalgic autobiographical narrative and overcoming a "divided self." Augustine is nostalgic for his "home" with God and for his *return* to rest in the "heavenly mansion" of his Father. By the same token, Wordsworth insists upon returning home—literally, after the French Revolution, and figuratively, in his retrospective poetry—to overcome his own sense of self-division and to reclaim, at "home" again with "mother nature," his powers as a poet. For both writers the feeling of self "division" generates a complex kind of nostalgia, which in turn feeds the sense of self-division until, ideally, each has journeyed home along the *via memoria* of his narrative. Barthes's "home," on the other hand, is dispersed throughout his text. It resides in the very "rhetoric" of his fragmented narrative, and has its "bed" in the "imaginary" (95). "Home," as a figure for everything in the past that a writer seeks in his narrative to return to and recover, is dispersed in the present out of which his book is generated. Barthes's *Barthes* does not seek "a central core" for itself or for the self who is writing it. Rather, like Valéry's vast *Cahiers*, it seeks for the self a way to *remain* dispersed by diffracting it into textual fragments. The only "home" Barthes really professes is the "bed of the imaginary," which is his way of saying that "Barthes" is most at home in the activity of composing *Barthes*.

We have seen that, in one form or another, the problematic status of the subject in self-reflexive literature has been a topic *of* that literature since Augustine's meditations in the *Confessions*, and we can understand Barthes's and Valéry's interest in that problematic as, in part, the repetition of an ongoing preoccupation that surfaces in Wordsworth, Carlyle, Proust, and

Adams. However, it is clear that in the substance and form of the two twentieth-century works, we confront both epistemological and literary disjunctions that have their roots in a particular historical moment. For as Barthes insisted, his book is different from earlier "confessions . . . because we have a different knowledge today" from the "old authors," because we "speak today of a divided subject" in ways much more complex than the "simple contradictions" of "yesterday."

Two points are of special interest in Barthes's and Valéry's preoccupation with this "different knowledge": the *knowledge* they articulate in their texts about writing and subjectivity *and* the way in which both writers seek to accommodate the *form* of their texts to that knowledge. In the act of this accommodation, the fragmented form of each work becomes a conscious image on the representational plane of the breakdown of an old epistemology of the literary and psychological subjects, a textual adjustment to the emergence of a new conception of the self as "heaped together" from "dispersed" fragments—in Nietzsche's words, a self "invented and projected behind what there is." The inventive and projective qualities of their self-reflexive writing are obvious, but the fragmented and discursive nature of their texts differs from the kind of invention and projection characteristic of a Joycean or a Proustian autobiographical novel. All four writers have fashioned their autobiographical works under the influence of changing ideas about the self and its literary representation, but each has accommodated his text to this new knowledge in different ways. While the works of Barthes and Valéry do not necessarily represent an *advance* over, say, Wordsworth or Joyce, they do represent a more conscious, and consciously disruptive response to a new epistemology that has, in fact, become thematized in twentieth-century literature. Their clear link to the Carlyle of *Sartor Resartus* should itself suggest how the self-reflexive strategies of Barthes and Valéry repeat and recapitulate as much as they inaugurate and originate. If there *is* anything like an advance represented by the *Cahiers* and *Roland Barthes*, it is in the realm of a heightened self-consciousness about the form of their texts. For what most emphatically separates their works from the other self-reflexive works treated in this study (and what, conversely, links them to *Sartor*) is the willfulness of their efforts to create a discursive form that itself clearly registers, indeed, embodies, a "new knowledge" of the subject. While an awakening to this knowledge disturbs the surface of *The Prelude* and *Four Quartets*, for example, that knowledge is willfully foregrounded in *Roland Barthes*, so that what once merely disturbed now becomes a structural principle.

With their biographies (in the conventional sense) less central to Valéry's and Barthes's conceptions of the "self" than was the case for Wordsworth, Joyce, or Proust, the *narrativity* of their works necessarily had to give way to a non-totalizing kind of *discourse*. For once the idea of selfhood becomes disengaged from biography, the autobiographical text can no longer be simply a story, but, as we have seen, must unfold in a more elliptical and purely discursive way. For authors such as Augustine or Wordsworth, who are trying in the composition of their works to "unify" themselves with an absent but somehow more "authentic" past self, a narrative *about* their pasts is a necessary kind of construction. But the belatedness they experience as they constuct it always puts its ability to help them achieve the kind of recovery they seek just out of reach. A *discursive* mode, on the other hand, which fully situates the writer's self in the moments of its composition in his text, seeks to avoid the ontological contradiction in autobiographical narration between the writer and his subject, while it also represents the abandonment of the kind of therapeutic hope we saw in Augustine, Wordsworth, and Proust. Whether such a discursive mode, wedded as we have seen it to be to a philosophical rather than a biographical examination, can be more truthful about the self than a narrative mode is another matter. For it may be that Barthes and Valéry have simply found ways to register more carefully and self-consciously the unavoidable ironies of self-representation that always render suspect its value as truth. They may both seek, in their abandonment of narrative and biography, to avoid Eliot's double need to bail himself out of his own past *and* his own poem. However, while the tension in Eliot's poem between historicity and discursiveness finds a kind of resolution in Valéry and Barthes, it should be emphasized that such a resolution is representational, and not necessarily psychological or spiritual.[9]

Narrative, especially in its Augustinian or Wordsworthian forms, implies the kind of nostalgia that Barthes's text seeks to disavow. The story told by a narrative in a self-reflexive work is always in some sense the story of a Proustian paradise, a paradise that the writer has already lost and, for Barthes, such a story ends by affirming that loss. Hence, his effort is to develop a literary mode in which he can write about himself in and for the present. His rejection of biography as content is at the same time a rejection of narrative as the proper literary mode for such an effort. In this way the self-reflexive textual strategy he pursues consciously shifts the ground of autobiographical practice—by way of an analytic, rather than a retrospective, meditation—in ways even more radical than the fictional methods of novelists such as Joyce and Proust. His book constitutes a kind of "autobiography" that in fact explodes the form of autobiography itself, since "Barthes" is written into his text *as* a disappropriated subject in a way that radically (and appropriately) deconstructs its very shape. A modern text like Barthes's, however, does not necessarily, as Michael Sprinker has sug-

9. As Jean Starobinski has pointed out in "The Style of Autobiography," reprinted in Olney, *Autobiography: Essays Theoretical and Critical* (73–83), discourse and history have always together informed the style of autobiography. What I am arguing here is that discourse stylistically—and strategically—overwhelms personal history in the three texts in question.

gested, constitute the "end" of autobiography, since people will no doubt continue to write quite traditional ones.[10] But it is a representation of a particular end to which it has come. As puzzling as its literary form and its ideas about writing and subjectivity may be, *Roland Barthes*, in its self-consciousness about its self-reflexivity, simply foregrounds and makes explicit problems and questions that have had a presence in autobiographical works since Augustine.

If the writer's transposition of himself into a self-reflexive literary text always involves a kind of struggle—as the works of Augustine, Wordsworth, Proust, Adams, and Eliot all affirm—that struggle itself becomes privileged as a productive, creative nexus in *Roland Barthes*. The "self" in this work is generated in a confrontation between the writer and his *ideas*, and it is out of this confrontation that "Barthes" emerges:

> His "ideas" have some relation to modernity . . . but he resists his ideas: his "self" or ego, a rational concretion, ceaselessly resists them. Though consisting apparently of a series of "ideas," this book is not the book of his ideas; it is the book of the Self, the book of my resistances to my own ideas . . . [119]

Barthes's stress on confrontation and resistance and on the role of language in the composition of his autobiographical subject links his text to the others in this study whose words "strain, crack and sometimes break, under the burden" of writing about

10. See Michael Sprinker, "Fictions of the Self: The End of Autobiography," in Olney, *Autobiography: Essays Theoretical and Critical*, 321–42. Sprinker's essay is a fine discussion of the ends to which the idea of autobiography and the self-reflexive subject have come after Nietzsche, Freud, Foucault, and Lacan. Sprinker's conclusion—that "autobiography . . . is always circumscribed by the limiting conditions of writing" (342)—goes to the heart of what my own study has tried to show. I cannot resist pointing out the meaningful pun in "circumscribe"—given the context in which Sprinker uses it—for the scribe in any autobiography is indeed surrounded on all sides by the limiting conditions of his activity, while that activity is in turn surrounded by the specter of the scribe (the subject) himself.

themselves, the burden of being *in* the text. Barthes discovers, with Augustine, that "man's understanding is spendthrift of words, because searching speaks more than does finding" and because "the hand that knocks is busier than the hand that receives." In this tension between narrative and discourse and in the wider kinds of problems with which this book has been concerned, the self-reflexive text can be observed both confronting and resisting that search. The variety of textual strategies that we have examined testify both to the writer's resiliency in the face of such a confrontation and to language's uncanny ability to lure him again and again into its web.

Index

Abrams, M. H., 40, 96
Adams, Henry:
  *The Degradation of the Democratic
    Dogma*, 157n29
  The Education of Henry Adams,
    153–160: and Augustine's
    Confessions, 153–156; as
    autobiography, 19; form of, 37;
    and modernism, 157–159;
    nature of protagonist in, 157;
    and *Sartor Resartus*, 154,
    156
Anderson, Chester G., 122n12
Augustine, St., 166, 171, 174
  Confessions, 29–32, 36, 45–46,
    146, 158, 161; as allegory,
    31; and *The Education of
    Henry Adams*, 153–156; form
    of, 24; and *Four Quartets*,
    169–171; and *The Prelude*,
    40–41, 56; and *Roland
    Barthes*, 176; as self-analysis,
    23–25
  See also Autobiographical literature
    as self-analysis; Autobiograph-
    ical literature, writing of, and
    self-transformation; Journey
    motif

Autobiographical literature:
  biography's role in, 162–164, 181
  deconstruction in, 174–183;
    and fiction, 16–17, 35–36,
    113, 115–116
  figure of editor in, 101
  fragmented forms of, 37–38, 65–
    66, 101–103, 165–167,
    175–176, 179
  generic definitions of, 14–21,
    93–94
  mimetic function of, 167
  narrative forms of, 36–37, 93–94,
    111–112, 118, 141, 152–156,
    158–160, 162–163, 166, 180–
    182
  nature of the subject in, 18 (*see
    also* Self, theories about,
    impact on autobiographical
    forms)
  and philosophy, 162
  referential status of, 18
  as self-analysis, 22, 30–32, 58–59,
    64, 68 (*See also* Psychoanaly-
    sis)
  writing of, and self-transformation,
    23–24, 26–27, 33–34, 36,
    53–56, 71–72, 74–75, 79–80,

Autobiographical literature (*cont.*)
  writing of, and self-transformation
    107, 120–122, 126, 149, 180
    (*see also* Psychoanalysis)

Barthes, Roland:
  Roland Barthes by Roland Barthes,
    20, 27–28, 35, 174–183;
    and Augustine's *Confessions*,
    176; nostalgia in, 177–178;
    restoration in, 176
  See also Self, theories about
Benstock, Bernard, 151n15
Bildungsroman, 19, 114
Blasing, Mutlu Konuk, 159n34
Bloom, Harold, 74, 82
Booth, Wayne, 122n12
Boyle, Robert, 151n15
Brisman, Leslie, 46
Bruss, Elizabeth W., 14n1
Burke, Kenneth, 32n21

Carlyle, Thomas, 110, 141
  and Henry Adams, 154
  Sartor Resartus, 20, 27, 28, 34–35,
    92–108, 115, 142, 152, 158,
    159, 162, 179; as auto-
    biography, 99–100; and *The
    Education of Henry Adams*,
    156; as an enabling work, 105–
    107; form of, 96–98; as
    parody, 96–97, 107; and *A
    Portrait of the Artist as a
    Young Man*, 35, 118, 126, 140;
    and *The Prelude*, 34–35,
    94–98, 101–102, 108, 112
  See also Self, theories about
Casey, Edward, 78
Christian model of fall and redemp-
    tion, 40n3; in *Four Quartets*,
    169–171; in *The Prelude*, 48;
    in Romantic poetry, 46; in
    Sartor Resartus, 96
Cixous, Hélène, 119n4, 120n7,
    128n22

Coleridge, Samuel Taylor, 62n28
Cooper, John C., 24n12
Creative process, theory of: in *A la
    recherche du temps perdu*,
    144–146; 148; in Hegel, 42–45;
    in *A Portrait of the Artist
    as a Young Man*, 120–122, 139
Croce, Benedetto, 109
Culler, Jonathan, 20
Curran, C.P., 119n5

Darbishire, Helen, 63
Death as a metaphor: in Adams, 158–
    159; in *A la recherche du
    temps perdu*, 36, 144–146; in
    *A Portrait of the Artist as a
    Young Man*, 36, 135, 143–144
Deleuze, Gilles, 148n10
De Man, Paul, 17–18, 83n17, 91
De Selincourt, Ernest, 60

Eliot, T. S., 176
  Four Quartets, 27, 35, 168–175;
    and Augustine's *Confessions*,
    37, 169–171; and *Cahiers*,
    37; deferring in, 171–172;
    discursive form of, 168;
    exploration in, 172–174; and
    The Prelude, 38; repetition in,
    170; time in, 171
Ellmann, Richard, 119n5, 121, 123,
    126–127, 139

Finch, John, 69
Flieger, Jerry Aline, 146–147
Forgetting: in *A la recherche du
    temps perdu*, 36, 146–148; in
    Nietzsche, 146; in *A Portrait
    of the Artist as a Young Man*, 36,
    142–143; in *The Prelude*,
    53, 83–87. *See also* Memory
Foucault, Michel, 110–113, 117
Franklin, Benjamin, 15–16, 166
Freud, Sigmund, 23, 74, 76;
    "Analysis Terminable and
    Interminable," 59, 64–65;

Freud, Sigmund (*cont.*)
"Beyond the Pleasure Principle,"
75; "Construction in Analysis,"
67n36; "Moses and Mono-
theism," 149; "New Introductory
Lectures," 75; "Wolf Man"
case history, 25. See also Autobiographical literature, as
self-analysis; Psychoanalysis

Glasheen, Adaline, 151n15
Goldberg, S. L., 125, 140

Haney, David P., 69n38
Harrold, Charles F., 99
Hartman, Geoffrey, 19, 39–42, 45–
46, 56–57, 80–81, 83n18,
88n21
Havens, Raymond, 76n6
Hawthorne, Nathaniel, *The Scarlet
Letter*, 17
Hegel, G. W. F., 42–45, 56, 73.
History, philosophy of, and
autobiographical forms, 108–114;
in Adams, 157n29; in Nietzsche,
35, 143; in Vico, 49

Jay, Gregory S., 169
Jones, John, 63n30
Journey motif: in Augustine's
Confessions, 33, 111; in *Four
Quartets*, 173; in *A Portrait
of the Artist as a Young Man*,
128; in *The Prelude*, 33, 46, 59,
62, 89, 97, 111; in *Sartor
Resartus*, 97
Joyce, James, 17, 159
and Carlyle, 126
and Catholicism, 126–127
Finnegans Wake, 151
and Hegel, 126
and Nietzsche, 116–117
*A Portrait of the Artist as a Young
Man*, 16, 19, 35, 115–144, 166;
aesthetic distance in, 122–123;

and *A la recherche du temps
perdu*, 142–153; and
Catholicism, 136; composition
of, 118–122, 125, 127, 150;
as an enabling work, 123–124,
140; and Nietzsche, 113–114;
and *The Prelude*, 35–36,
115–118, 123–124; pro-
tagonists's development as a
writer in, 131–140; and *Sartor
Resartus*, 35, 118, 140
Stephen Hero, 118–119, 121,
125, 150
Ulysses, 139–140
See also Forgetting

Kain, Richard M., 119n2, 127n21
Kierkegaard, Sören, 79

Lacan, Jacques, 26
Langbaum, Robert, 95n6, 96n7
Language, role of: in Augustine's
Confessions, 30–31, 32n21; in
Four Quartets, 168–171;
in *A Portrait of the Artist as a
Young Man*, 127–140; in *The
Prelude*, 46, 50–51, 81–82; in
psychoanalysis, 26; in
Wordsworth's poetic theory,
47–50
LaValley, Albert J., 95n6, 97, 98, 99,
105–106
Lindenberger, Herbert, 76n6, 77
Loss: in *A la recherche du temps
perdu*, 147–148; in *Cahiers*,
165; in *The Prelude*, 80–81; in
Roland Barthes, 181

Magalaner, Marvin, 119n2, 127n21
Mehlman, Jeffrey, 18
Memory: in *A la recherche du temps
perdu*, 36, 146–148; in
Augustine's *Confessions*, 30–31;
in *Cahiers*, 164–165; in
Four Quartets, 168, 173; in

Memory (cont.)
    Freud, 25–26; in *A Portrait of
    the Artist as a Young Man*,
    120, 142–144; in *The Prelude*,
    36, 52–54, 66–67, 78–79,
    85, 87; in *Roland Barthes*, 175.
    See also Forgetting
Moore, Carlisle, 106

Nietzsche, Friedrich, 45, 142, 146,
    152, 159, 175, 179; and
    Joyce, 116–117; *The Use and
    Abuse of History*, 109–114;
    The Will to Power, 28. *See also*
    History, philosophy of; Self,
    theories about

Olney, James, 14–15, 167n4, 173n6
Onorato, Richard, 81n14
Origins, search for, 111–113, 117; in
    The Prelude, 46–50, 58

Parrish, Stephen, 60, 67, 69–70
Pascal, Roy, 14n1
Peckham, Morse, 95, 99
Pine-Coffin, R. S., 24n12
Proust, Marcel, 17, 159
    A la recherche du temps perdu, 19,
        23, 35, 141; as an enabling
        work, 145–146; interpretation
        in, 148; and *A Portrait of the
        Artist as a Young Man*,
        142–153
    Contre Saint-Beuve, 150
    Jean Santeuil, 149
    The Past Recaptured, 36; and *The
        Prelude*, 36
    See also Death as a metaphor;
        Forgetting; Memory
Psychoanalysis, 21–27, 58–59, 64–65,
    67, 75, 149; and narrative
    autobiography, 24–27. *See also*
    Autobiographical literature,
    as self-analysis; Freud, Sigmund;
    Lacan, Jacques

Reed, Mark, L., 60n22
Romanticism and religion, 39–42,
    45–46
Rousseau, Jean-Jacques, *The
    Confessions*, 19–20, 155
Ryan, John K., 32n21

Said, Edward W., 65n35, 123–
    124, 141
Samuels, Ernest, 153–154
Sayre, Robert F., 156
Scholes, Robert, 122n12
Self, and other: in *A la recherche du
    temps perdu*, 36; in *Cahiers*,
    167–168; in *Four Quartets*, 170;
    in *A Portrait of the Artist as
    a Young Man*, 116
Self, divided: 37; in Augustine's
    Confessions, 178
Self, theories about: in Adams, 156–
    158; in Barthes, 38, 177, 182;
    in Carlyle, 27, 95, 104–105, 156;
    in Hegel, 45; impact on auto-
    biographical forms, 21–22,
    27–38, 41–42, 97–98, 103–105,
    107–108, 112, 116–118, 140,
    151–152, 159, 161–166,
    175–176, 178–183; in Nietzsche,
    28–29; in Valéry, 37. *See
    also* Autobiographical literature,
    fragmented forms of; narrative
    forms of
Shakespeare, William, 139
Shattuck, Roger, 150
Shumaker, Wayne, 93–94
Spanos, William V., 169
Spencer, Theodore, 119n1
Spengemann, William C., 14n1, 17,
    42n5, 98n16, 99, 105
Sprinker, Michael, 181–182
Starobinski, Jean, 181

Tennyson, G. B., 99
Todorov, Tzvetan, 20

Valéry, Paul:
   Cahiers, 20; as autobiography,
      163–164
   "La Jeune Parque," 167n4
   "Propos me concernant," 163–168
   See also Self, theories about
Van Ghent, Dorothy, 128n22
Vico, Giambattista, 49–50

White, Hayden, 109–110
Whitman, Walt, 113
Wordsworth, William, 149, 166
   essay on "Poetic Diction," 46–48
      and Hegel, 44–46
   Preface to *Lyrical Ballads*, 48
   The Prelude, 15–16, 19, 20, 23, 26,
      28, 32–34, 92–93, 142,
      146, 162, 174; and Augustine's
      Confessions, 40–41, 56;
      chronology in, 54, 62–65, 67,
      80; composition of, 22,
      59–72, 76; cyclical form of,
   50–55; as an enabling
      work, 48–50, 55n18, 58, 124;
      and modernism, 93; and
      Past Recaptured, 36; and *A
      Portrait of the Artist as a
      Young Man*, 35–36, 123–124;
      repetition in, 74–80; theme
      of restoration in, 53–56,
      71–72, 74–75, 79–80, 91; late
      revisions of, 63–65; and
      Sartor Resartus, 34–35, 94–
      98, 101–102, 108, 112
   The Recluse, 63, 68, 70, 73
   "The Thorn," 77
   "Tintern Abbey," 52n16.
   and Vico, 49–50
   See also Christian model of fall and
      redemption; Forgetting;
      Journey motif; Language, role
      of; Memory; Origins, search
      for
Wright, Frank Lloyd, 16

Library of Congress Cataloging in Publication Data

JAY, PAUL, 1946–
    Being in the text.

    Includes bibliographical references and index.
      1. Literature, Modern—19th century–History and
criticism.   2. Literature, Modern–20th century—
History and criticism.   3. Authors in literature.
4. Autobiography.   5. Fiction, Autobiographic.
I. Title.
PN761.J39   1983   809′.93353   82-45145
ISBN 0-8014-1599-3 (alk. paper)